DATE DUE

DEMCO 38-296

Information Literacy

Proceedings of the Twenty-eighth Annual
Symposium of the Graduate Alumni and Faculty
of the Rutgers School of Communication,
Information and Library Studies, 6 April 1990

Information Literacy: Learning How to Learn

Edited by Jana Varlejs

McFarland & Company, Inc., Publishers
Jefferson, North Carolina, and London

This is the ninth in a McFarland series of Rutgers SCILS symposia under the general editorship of Jana Varlejs. The first eight are *The Economics of Information* (1982), *The Right to Information* (1984), *Communication/Information/Libraries* (1985), *Freedom of Information and Youth* (1986), *Information Seeking* (1987), *Information and Aging* (1988), *Leadership in the Library/Information Profession* (1989), and *Information Ethics* (1990).

British Library Cataloguing-in-Publication data are available

Library of Congress Cataloguing-in-Publication Data

Information literacy : learning how to learn : proceedings of the
   twenty-eighth annual symposium of the graduate alumni and faculty of
   the Rutgers School of Communication, Information and Library
   Studies, 6 April 1990 / edited by Jana Varlejs.
      p. cm.
   Includes bibliographical references.
   ISBN 0-89950-617-8 (sewn softcover : 55# alk. paper) ∞
   1. Library orientation—Congresses. 2. Information services—User
education—Congresses. 3. Information technology—Study and
teaching—Congresses. I. Varlejs, Jana. II. Rutgers University.
School of Communication, Information and Library Studies.
Z711.2.I48   1991
025.5′6—dc20   91-52595
                                                            CIP

Manufactured in the United States of America

McFarland & Company, Inc., Publishers
  Box 611, Jefferson, North Carolina 28640

Dedication

EDWARD J. BLOUSTEIN
1925–1989

As President of Rutgers, The State University of New Jersey, from 1971 to 1989, Edward Bloustein led the University through a time of reorganization, diversification, and enormous growth, and took great satisfaction in seeing Rutgers join the ranks of the major research universities. Under his leadership, the present School of Communication, Information and Library Studies was formed, and he took a personal interest in its evolution. In his introductory remarks at the twenty-second annual symposium in 1983, he spoke about his own involvement in a computerized information network and the awe he experienced in realizing the power of such scholarly communication technology. He did not have a specific agenda for the School in mind, but he did have a vision of its potential for forging exciting new interdisciplinary pursuits. He expected the School to succeed, and challenged us to make our very best effort. We value his confidence in us, respect his contribution to First Amendment scholarship (see *The Right to Information,* McFarland, 1984), and admire his farsighted leadership.

Distinguished Alumni Award

The annual symposium of the graduate alumni and faculty of the Rutgers School of Communication, Information and Library Studies is the occasion for adding the name of a distinguished graduate to the roll of individuals who have brought honor to the School through their achievements. The 1990 symposium followed this custom by honoring Karen Takle Quinn for her exemplary career in information science. The citation presented to her on April 6 read as follows:

TRIBUTE TO KAREN TAKLE QUINN

Whereas Karen Takle Quinn has been an innovator who pioneered in special library automation and created a model integrated library/computer information/learning center, and

Whereas Karen Takle Quinn has provided an exemplary internship program for library and information science students, has taught state-of-the-art technology and management courses in MLS programs, and has contributed to the literature of librarianship, information science, engineering, and office automation, and

Whereas Karen Takle Quinn has assumed increasingly demanding assignments during her twenty-five year career with IBM, ranging from international marketing to new product planning, and has forged new career paths in the corporate environment for other librarians as well, and

Whereas Karen Takle Quinn has been active in a wide range of information and engineering professional societies, and has been elected Fellow of the Institute of Information Scientists,

Therefore, be it resolved, that the Rutgers Graduate Alumni of the School of Communication, Information and Library Studies honors Karen Takle Quinn as the Distinguished Alumna of the Year 1990, and

Be it further resolved that this distinction be spread upon the minutes of this Association and be made known to the library and information science community.

Table of Contents

Acknowledgments

The assistance of alumni Luis Rodriguez and Janet Simkin and faculty members Betty Turock and Dan O'Connor in planning and logistics are especially appreciated. Peggy Hoydis did her usual excellent job of transcription, and Ruth Picker smoothed the editing process. IBM's support of travel expenses was most welcome. For the thorough work on preparing a bibliography to accompany these proceedings, we are indebted to Howard Dess. Above all, we thank the speakers for thoughtful and provocative presentations.

Information Literacy:
Just Another Buzzword?

Jana Varlejs

What *is* information literacy? Is it simply the latest buzzword in librarianship, or is it an apt expression of the evolving role of the information profession today?

The publication of the report of the American Library Association's Presidential Committee on Information Literacy in 1989 marked the codification of the concept, although the basic ideas encompassed have been around for a long time (see the bibliography starting on page 63). The Committee defined the concept as follows:

> To be information literate, a person must be able to recognize when information is needed and have the ability to locate, evaluate, and use effectively the needed information. ... Ultimately, information literate people are those who have learned how to learn. They know how to learn because they know how knowledge is organized, how to find information, and how to use information in such a way that others can learn from them. They are people prepared for lifelong learning, because they can always find the information needed for any task or decision at hand (page 1).

While the report deals with the inportance of information in business and for citizenship, it places the greatest emphasis on the need to overhaul schooling at all levels. The objective would be to have students learn actively through the use of resources and information gathering and analysis, rather than passively through texts and workbooks. The library would become central, rather than peripheral to learning.

The report concludes with recommendations which deal mainly

with building coalitions and raising public awareness. There is an implicit recognition that the library profession cannot make a dent in information illiteracy without the cooperation of educators.

Until the day when the education establishment accepts and acts upon the challenge to integrate the learning-how-to-learn approach into curricula, what can librarians do on their own? No single answer emerges from these papers presented at the Rutgers symposium on information literacy.

Carol Kuhlthau urges librarians to put less stress on teaching traditional library skills, and more on facilitating the process of using and evaluating information resources across the curriculum. The emphasis should be on the process rather than on the tools, and the result should be critical thinking rather than rote learning.

Karen Takle Quinn suggests that librarians serving business and industry should lead the way in exploiting new information technology to help their clients to keep up with their constant need to learn new skills. As demands are placed on the work force to become increasingly sophisticated in applying information to problem solving and decision making, the library/information specialist should select and help in the use of computer-assisted self-paced learning systems.

Prudence Dalrymple believes that much better system design is needed in order to give more effective access to information resources. Using online public access library catalogs as an example, she faults our tendency to create systems which may serve the convenience of librarians, but which stymie the library user.

Charles Curran, on the other hand, implies that our major effort should not go into making people self-sufficient information system users. Rather, we should concentrate on insuring successful encounters with user-friendly librarians who can provide the information sought.

Major Owens concurs, referring to his own reliance on the Congressional Research Service. On the other hand, he has a vision of library service at the community level which would foster grass roots information literacy through "family learning centers."

During the discussion period, presenters and audience seemed to come to a consensus of sorts. Yes, it is important to help people to become information literate, but librarians should be more willing to do the job on behalf of their clients. There also seemed to be agreement with Curran's judgment that information literacy is a more holistic concept than bibliographic instruction, and that it means an expanded role for librarians.

What remained less clear was exactly what that expanded role should be. Several comments touched on the need for librarians to assume responsibility for evaluating information as well as for helping their clients learn to become critical information consumers. Major Owens saw the implications of this: we need more staff, and more highly differentiated staffing patterns.

As Pat Schuman points out in her introduction, the symposium presented an opportunity to learn how to think about the problem of information literacy. For me, several lines of thought do emerge from the papers and discussion, and all need to be pursued vigorously. First, we can and must jettison stand-alone models of library skills/bibliographic instruction, and replace them with curriculum-integrated process models. Second, we can and must do a better job of information systems design to make it more congruent with what we know about people's information seeking behaviors. Third, we can and must incorporate self-paced, computer-assisted learning technology into our libraries. Fourth, we can and must revise library education so as to produce librarians who practice information analysis and who take professional responsibility for the *information* they provide — not just references to the sources. Fifth, we must stop being so modest about the value and importance of the role of librarians in achieving national educational and productivity goals, and must demand the resources we need to do the job that we are uniquely qualified to do.

None of these ideas are new, just as the concept of information literacy is not really new. Perhaps "information literacy" will turn out to be just another buzzword that will quickly lose whatever potency it has. For the moment, however, we can use this concept as a unifying, clarifying construct: to identify ourselves as a profession, to define our social role, and to design a concerted campaign to realize our vision of an information literate citizenry.

Introduction

Patricia Glass Schuman

I recently came across a quote from Oscar Wilde that I really like because it exemplifies where we are today in the prevention of information illiteracy. When asked about the opening of his new play, he said to a friend: "the play was a great success but the audience was a failure." When we talk about literacy today we are talking about the same kind of problem. It is said that we are living in an information society—a knowledge society, a society powered by information. That's a fantasy. The fantasy goes something like this: we are in the midst of an information explosion and our only hope for controlling it is through the use of technology. New technology will provide users with greater access than ever before. Individuals will easily and directly access information to fill their needs from their homes and their offices through their computers.

The statistics about information are dramatic, certainly. Last year Americans bought 13.2 million tons of newspapers; over a million books are published annually—over a thousand books a day world-wide. A weekly edition of the *New York Times* contains more information than the average person was likely to come across in a lifetime in seventeenth-century England. The English language now contains 500,000 words, five times more than in Shakespeare's lifetime. The collection of the large research libraries has doubled in the last fourteen years. We readily throw out with our nightly garbage more print than past generations dreamed it was possible to own.

But what do these statistics really dramatize? They tell us that there is more data than ever before, not that there is better data, more relevant information, or even a more knowledgeable society. A typical newspaper, after all, is more than 60 percent ads. A typical American reads three books a year. What we are actually experiencing is not an information explosion — it is an explosion of data. Some scientists now claim that it takes less time to do an experiment than to find out whether it has been done before. Richard Saul Wurman, author of *Information Anxiety* (Doubleday, 1989), calls what has been happening the non-information explosion. Data by itself provides neither information nor knowledge. Words like misinformation, disinformation, meaning-glut and info-lag are becoming commonplace. Some have described the situation as access to excess. The fact that there is more data available does not mean that people want it or use it meaningfully.

An individual must be literate in order to negotiate our complex social, political, economic, and work environments, but print illiteracy is almost a national disease. Twenty-three million Americans can't read above the fifth grade level. Twenty percent of all Americans can't even write a check that a bank can process. And an individual must not only be print literate, he or she must be culturally literate, visually literate, and computer literate. With all these skills, the individual might then have a shot at being information literate. And an educated user also needs the awareness of the value of information, and the financial wherewithall to use it. You may talk about the home delivery of information. What does that really mean in a society where 25 percent of households below the poverty line have no telephone? PC's are now in only 13 percent of U.S. households; only 10 percent of these have modems. Seventeen percent of all white children use a computer at home; only 6 percent of black and hispanic children do. Rather than universal delivery, there is a very real possibility that the gap between the information rich and the information poor is widening.

Meetings like this one hopefully will help us learn how to learn how to help the information poor, the nonusers as well as the users of libraries and information centers. When Albert Einstein was asked what was the greatest contribution in helping him come up with the theory of relativity, he is said to have answered, figuring out how to think about the problem. That's our challenge today.

Bringing Up an Information Literate Generation: Dynamic Roles for School and Public Libraries

Carol C. Kuhlthau

The underlying question in information literacy is: What does it mean to be literate in the information age? Certainly children need to know how to read, to communicate ideas in writing and orally, to calculate numbers. Beyond these traditional skills of literacy, what unique abilities are needed for everyday life in an information society, particularly in the information workplace? This paper will explore this question and address the role of libraries in developing information literacy in children.

The American Library Association (ALA) Presidential Committee on Information Literacy, of which I was a member, defined information literacy as being able to recognize when information is needed, and to have the ability to locate, evaluate and use the information needed. These abilities are applied to learning from information throughout one's life. Our final report addressed the importance of information literacy in individuals' lives, in business, and for citizenship.[1] Information literacy is a survival skill in the information age. There is a very real danger of becoming a nation divided between those who have the ability to learn from information and those who do not.

New technologies have drastically altered the workplace and the skills needed to be competent on the job. In her book, *The Age of the Smart Machine,* Shoshana Zuboff describes her study of the effects of transition to an automated workplace on three types of workers: executives, plant workers, and office workers.[2] She reports that all three groups are required to make more critical judgments and to apply more abstract thinking in an automated work environment. Decisions made on the job require using computer-generated information rather than information gathered from direct personal contact with the problem situation. The automated workplace also requires less individualized tasks and more team projects. She suggests that ability to make critical judgments from abstract information and ability to work as a member of a team are essential skills for the information age workplace. These abilities converge in actual work situations where critical judgments are made by teams of workers.

If we examine how school learning has been structured it is not surprising that students are not prepared for the information workplace. Schools have been organized on an industrial model which ironically has been intensified by recent attempts to increase accountability. For one thing, most instruction has centered around predigested material in textbooks and has been directed to simple "right" answers which can be tested, measured, and compared across population. "Teaching for the test" has become common practice in many of our schools rather than encouraging creative, innovative thinking and offering opportunities for developing ability in making critical judgments. In addition, competition between students has been emphasized rather than teaming in a cooperative process of learning.

Educating an information literate generation calls for restructuring schools in some very basic ways. While the library has the potential for dynamically contributing to this restructuring, none of the many recent K–12 reports on education has explored the potential role of libraries. This is particularly disappointing in light of the fact that for at least twenty years the school library has been referred to as the center or the "hub" of the school. This is an idea that's time has come. The library as the information center is a critical component for preparing children for the information age.

An information age school is described in the report on information literacy as follows:

> The school would be more interactive, because students, pursuing questions of personal interest would be interacting with other students, with teachers, with a vast array of information resources, and the community at large to a far greater degree than they presently do today. One would expect to find every student engaged in at least one open-ended, long-term quest for an answer to a serious social, scientific, aesthetic, or political problem. Students' quests would involve not only searching print, electronic, and video data, but also inter-

viewing people inside and outside of school. As a result, learning would be more self-initiated. There would be more reading of original sources and more extended writing. Both students and teachers would be familiar with the intellectual and emotional demands of asking productive questions, gathering data of all kinds, reducing and synthesizing information, and analyzing, interpreting, and evaluating information in all its forms. ... One would expect such a school to look and sound different from today's schools. ... On the playground, in the halls, in the cafeteria, and certainly in the classroom, one would hear fundamental questions that make information literacy so important: How do you know that? and What evidence do you have for that? Who says? and How can we find out?[3]

What is the dynamic role of the library in educating children to become information literate? There are several significant contributions librarians make in the information age school. The first is a knowledge of resources. Literacy in the information age requires that classroom instruction be grounded in multiple resources rather than bound to a single textbook. The librarian provides access to a wealth of materials rich in challenging ideas, fully integrated with the curriculum. In resource-based learning, as advocated in *Information Power,* the AASL/AECT guidelines for school library media programs, the librarian and the teacher work together as a team to plan instruction and to teach students in all areas across the curriculum using the resources of the library media center.[4] The librarian's knowledge of resources combines a wide variety of wonderful books to read with both technology for instruction and technology for accessing information.

The second significant contribution librarians make in the information age school is a knowledge of process. The process of learning from information is at the core of an information literacy program. The information search process is a complex learning process in which new constructs are formed as information is encountered. My own research into the users' perspective of information seeking has shown that people experience uncertainty in the early stages of learning from information which often leads to anxiety and frustration.[5] New information is inconsistent and in conflict with what we already know. Once a personal perspective has been constructed through reading and reflecting, we feel more confident as well as more interested in our pursuit. Students need guidance in the process of information seeking, particularly through those early stages, in order to develop confidence and competence in information seeking and use.

The knowledge of resources and process fosters a broader view of library skills. Information skills are not limited to learning how to use a particular library or a specific source. Rather, the library is a laboratory for learning the concepts of information location and use. The concept of organization, indexing, and access are taught using such tools as the Dewey Decimal System, card catalog and *Readers' Guide* as examples. The library also serves as a laboratory for learning how to use information for finding out about the world. Information skills are process skills similar to those of reading and writing. Just as children need something to read and to write about, they need a reason to use information, something to think about and to learn. These skills are not taught in isolation. The library plays a critical role in enabling them to use information after it is located. Children are guided in recognizing when they need information — which is crucial; in making sense of what they have found; fitting it in with what they already know; and seeking further information based on expanding thoughts.

What does a library program centered on information literacy look like?

Information literacy is not taught as a separate course but is integrated with learning across the curriculum. The program is designed for all students, not just the college bound, and is developed around the basic need of every person to find meaning and understand his or her world. A team teaching approach is employed in which the teacher brings knowledge of content and concepts and the librarian brings knowledge of resources and process.

In the field studies I have been conducting over the past eight years, a consistent pattern is emerging of a natural sequence of information use activites.[6] This sequence matches both children's developmental stages and their need for information arising from their classrooms and their personal lives. A sequential information environment can be planned for students from elementary, through middle, and high school.

Children in kindergarten through fifth or sixth grade are involved in expanding their knowledge base and in learning to read, write, and communicate ideas. During this time they need to interact with lots of books and the ideas generated in books and other materials. Electronic technology for gathering and processing ideas need to be readily available. Activities center on developing skill in using information by having children recall (tell what they remember), summarize (tell in a capsulized form), paraphrase (tell in their own words), and extend (tell their reaction and how this relates to what they already know). Instruction centers around inquiry and discovery with children actively involved in their own learning and sharing that learning with their classmates. As questions arise and a need for more information is apparent, they are guided in finding out and sharing what they have found with their classmates. They are rewarded for telling in their own words, rather than copying out of a book, but also are encouraged to report the source of their information. In this way, children are continually engaged in recognizing their need for information and in locating, evaluating, and using information as a means of learning.

By middle school these children are ready to address an extensive problem requiring an extended search for information. A personally compelling question, topic, or issue motivates their sustained attention. Their ability to recall, summarize, paraphrase, and extend is applied to the task of writing a paper or other presentation. Their work focuses on their perspective formed during a period of concentrated information use under the guidance of the team of the librarian and the teachers. Collaboration and cooperation among students is encouraged. Students learn the process of locating, evaluating, and using information as well as the mechanics of producing a product to report their findings. The mechanics, however, do not overshadow their primary purpose of finding out and telling. They learn the interrelationship of information sources, such as how information gathered from interviewing an expert relates to that obtained from an organized collection. They learn ways of integrating information into what they already know and methods for documenting the origins of their emerging ideas. They use information technologies such as databases and become aware of vast networks of information. They are guided through the search process and reflect on their experience throughout. The process of seeking information as well as the product produced is assessed and evaluated.

In high school, assignments center on the process of learning from information. Students are actively involved in synthesizing, analyzing, drawing conclusions, identifying further questions and problems. They are challenged to integrate information from mass media and everyday life experience with classroom learning. As troubling or interesting questions arise they are expected to seek further information in the organized collection of the library. Findings are reported and presented in a variety of ways, some requiring extensive writing, others presented less formally, such as sharing an insight on a muddled point raised in class. Integrating past experience with new learning leads to evaluative analysis and critical judgments. Collaboration among students provides support in the process of information seeking as well as encouraging an exchange of ideas. A wide range of print and electronic resources are available, as well as access to networks of information outside of the school.

Restructuring schools for educating a generation prepared for the information workplace is a critical issue in education today. The library's dynamic role can not be fully realized without a clear perception by other key players in the school community. In 1987, the New Jersey State Library sponsored a three-day seminar for teams of teachers, administrators, librarians and school board members from thirty school districts. The purpose was to examine and develop the role of the school library in providing excellence in education for our children. I was asked to conduct a study of changes in perception of the role of the librarian over the course of the three days.[7] Although it is unusual to find any change in a short period of time, there was significant change in several areas. At the close of the conference, participants' perceptions of the library media specialist's role in curriculum planning and resource-based teaching had increased significantly. Board members began to think of librarians as more than keepers of the books. Administrators saw more active participation in integrating a multimedia collection into the curriculum and in developing curriculum. Teachers also held a broader view of librarians in curriculum development and in participating in the teaching of thinking skills. Library media specialists broadened their view of their role in instruction. The only objective considered less important by any group at the close of the conference was the library media specialists' shift on a question related to teaching library skills. During the conference the librarians began to view their instructional role more broadly and to consider thinking about information and problem solving as part of their role rather than concentrating completely on a more narrow view of library skills. Realization of the vast potential of the library media program for improving education became apparent to each group participating. Out of this initiative have come New Jersey guidelines for developing programs which are being field tested in schools across the state this spring.[8]

The library has a dynamic role in bringing up an information literate generation. At Rutgers, the Library and Information Studies Department has made a commitment to educate graduates to assume leadership roles. All of our students learn the complexity of information structure, technology, management, and human interaction. Those preparing to work with children and teenagers are given the challenge of translating this knowledge to programs promoting information literacy.

References

1. *American Library Association Presidential Committee on Information Literacy: Final Report* (Chicago: American Library Association, 1989).

2. Shoshana Zuboff. *The Age of the Smart Machine: The Future of Work and Power* (New York: Basic Books, 1988).

3. *Information Literacy: Final Report,* p. 8.

4. American Association of School Librarians and Association for Educational Communications and Technology, *Information Power: Guidelines for School Library Media Programs* (Chicago: American Library Association, 1988).

5. Carol C. Kuhlthau. "Developing a Model of a Library Search Process: Cognitive and Affective Aspects," *RQ* 28 (Winter 1989): 232–42.

6. Carol C. Kuhlthau. "Information Search Process: A Summary of Research and Implications for School Library Media Programs," *School Library Media Quarterly* 18 (Fall 1989): 19–25.

7. Carol C. Kuhlthau. "Objectives of the Library Media Center: A Study of Perceptions of School Administrators, Board Members, Teachers, and Librarians," *Emanations* 11 (Spring 1988): 7–9.

8. *Guidelines for School Library Media Centers* (Trenton: New Jersey State Library Development Bureau, 1990).

Information Literacy in the Workplace: Education/Training Considerations

Karen Takle Quinn

Introduction

Today there are serious threats facing business enterprises worldwide. Among the changes are: the emergence of aggressive global competitors; obsolete management practices and declining productivity; capacity excesses of competitors; product substitution; exploding technologies and higher R&D costs; customer demand for more performance, quality and lower prices. In order to survive we must become market driven and we must use information resources effectively.

Information will help us to identify market niches, make our employees more knowledgeable and productive, develop competitive advantages, have the right capabilities and cost structures, and achieve better implementation of results.

From 1959, when I finished my graduate degree at Rutgers, until today many changes have taken place. First our name: we are now called the Rutgers School of Communication, Information, and Library Studies. Our information perspectives have totally changed. Some may call this a paradigm shift.

Years ago when we thought about being "information literate," we spoke about the "effective use of libraries." Today technology offers us a wider range of information and communication resources. Often we have seen references to the three-stage shift from the agricultural society to an industrial society and into the information age. In the United States especially, the production, storage, and distribution of information has become the major activity of many workers.

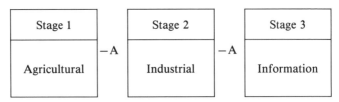
Figure 1. Evolution to the Information Age.

Quality and Productivity

Information resources became a focus of management in the 1980s. In each decade sine the early 1900s we have seen capital, people and materials resources become focus points of management. In the fifties we began to see an emphasis on the conservation of natural resources. In the sixties management's attention was directed at resource control. The seventies began with the Paperwork Simplification Act, and an emphasis (especially by the federal government) on the reduction of unnecessary paperwork and application of management principles to paperwork. In the eighties the information finally became recognized as a resource which needed to be managed just like other assets in a corporation or enterprise. The new position of Chief Information Officer appeared. In the nineties I believe the focus will be on the use of information for quality and productivity and greater profitability. This will put additional focus on information. This will also require all employees to be information literate. Information will be used not only to make decisions, but to target market niches, produce quality products, to make employees more knowledgeable and productive and thereby add to the profitability of their enterprises.

Today, we only need to look around our work and home environments to see how information technologies have changed these environments. The most apparent of these changes are:

- Images can be transferred via telephone lines and FAX machines. FAX telephone numbers are appearing on not only business stationery but home stationery as well. The FAX machine is becoming a common appliance.
- Many people are, or are becoming, computer literate.
- School children to executives are using word processors.
- Microcomputers are becoming a common appliance in offices and homes.
  - Have you been on a plane lately without someone working on a portable microcomputer?

—Do you know anyone who hasn't heard of LOTUS 1,2,3? They may not know how to run it or what it does exactly but surely they have heard the name or seen it mentioned in their local newspaper.

—Project management tools and other automated tools have greatly increased our information knowledge and capabilities.

How quickly our work and home environments have changed.

Changes in the Workplace Environment

We must recognize that CHANGE is the driving force of business. Clearly we are moving toward more highly technical and complex systems. In the workplace, we must assess our information needs and technology support to make certain we are in the best competitive position we can be. We need to examine the work environment to see that the information from multiple sources about the business is available when it is needed and in a form which provides the greatest added value. In addition we need to make certain that employees clearly understand how critical it is to the profitability goals of the enterprise (actually, in today's business environment, to their survival) that every employee be not only information literate but information knowledgeable: knowing not only what information exists but also how to make effective use of this information.

Change can also be seen as a result of today's worldwide economic shifts. These shifts will have a real variety of impacts on the job market and associated information needs.

If one takes a future-oriented look at jobs and organizations, already we see the globalization of markets. This again adds to the complexity of information. Employees will need to learn how to function with individuals from cultures around the world.

As technology complexity increases, we move from a procedural or and predictable set of tasks to a position where people become responsible for:

- understanding the real question
- looking for inferences
- making diagnoses
- making judgments based upon available information
- making decisions

all under severe time and pressure constraints.

History of the Management of Resources

Timeframe	Resource Focus
1900s Early	CAPITAL Resources
1930s	PEOPLE Resources
1940s	MATERIAL Resources
	(World War II Resources Scarce)
1950s	CONSERVATION OF NATURAL RESOURCES
	Beginning of Conservation of Natural Resources
1960s	RESOURCE CONTROL MANAGEMENT
1970s	PAPERWORK MANAGEMENT
1980s	INFORMATION MANAGEMENT
1990s	USE OF INFORMATION for Quality and Productivity
	and Profitability

Figure 2. History of Emphasis on Resources.

We know the demographics are changing for both the entry-level and the mature worker. We are moving from a manufacturing to a service orientation. Changes such as these have a great impact on the need for information literacy and the level of information literacy required.

Major policies, marketing and technology trends reshape information implementation and the marketplace itself. When new enabling technologies appear, how do they transform the distribution of information to business? Additionally, how will these innovations be integrated into the business environments? How will the implementation in a particular enterprise affect their productivity and global competitiveness? How will this change the information needs and flow?

What are the enabling technologies that will modify and transform the provision of information to the home? How will they be integrated into the consumer environment?

These are difficult and complex question. I am not attempting in this thirty-minute paper to provide the answers to these challenges. It is important that we as professionals recognize and consider the changes taking place. We need to think, analyze, and plan for this future with multiple solutions.

Example of New Technology Introduction

For example, on March 13, 1990, the IBM Corporation introduced the IBM ImagePlus High Performance Transaction System (HPTS).

This announcement includes many new products including processors, scanners, image processing, image-capture devices, hardware attached to IBM PS/2(tm)s, and new software. In addition, it builds upon existing software and hardware such as Local Area Networks (LANS), IBM DATABASE 2, and IBM Host Systems. HPTS captures and stores electronic images of documents, such as handwritten checks. When HPTS cannot read an image successfully, the document image is displayed on a PS/2(tm) workstation screen for the operator to enter the correct amount. After all the checks have been processed, HPTS provides the information that operators need to correct the out-of-balance condition at their workstation.

Today, these applications are banking oriented; but with the open-ended architecture, this product could be used for archive research, document processing, forecasting, credit card draft processing, return check processing, and other applications. What kind of information literacy does this entry level operator require? How will they learn "how to" operate in this high tech environment?

A set of "how-to" training lessons was announced with HPTS. These training tutorials use IBM MultiMedia solutions which is an interactive video system that brings together audio, motion, and video text and computer images and combines them on a touch sensitive screen. Now, with just the touch of a finger, employees can get actual hands-on experience during training. Instead of paper, pencils and chalk, IBM MultiMedia provides the capability to select and mix the latest high-impact video techniques, computer graphics, sound and brilliant photography to help people learn.

This type of training allows employees to increase their proficiency at one task or expand their skills to multiple tasks. These well-defined roles provide a logical job-growth path for the employees.

As technology shifts, so do jobs and the information related to the tasks of each job. In an April 14, 1987, article about a new car assembly plant in Michigan, the *Washington Post* reported that

> they want their new employees to be able to work in teams, to rotate through various jobs, to understand how their tasks fit into the entire process, to spot problems in production, to trouble shoot, articulate the problems to others, suggest improvements, and write detail charts and memos that serve as a road map in the assembly of the car.

Consider what this article reports as the work attitudes, level of understanding of the automobile production process, and the communication skills levels expected of these employees at this new assembly plant. What information will they need to do their jobs as expected? How will these employees be trained?

Factors Affecting Information Literacy Requirements

Enterprise Factors	Personal Characteristics	Task Considerations
Economic Success	Personality	Level of Complexity
Market-Share in the Industry	Cognitive Style	Information Sources
Economic Health of the Industry in the Global Market Place	Human Bias	Difficulty
Management Style	Motivation	Importance
Organizational Structure	Attitudes	Newness
Level of Information Technology	Expectations	Uncertainty
Timeframe to Implement Change	Training	Time Available to Accomplish
Priorities	Experience	Knowledge
Internal Power & Politics	Adaptability	Documentation Quality
Attitude Toward Information	Reading Comprehension	Method of Data Entry

Figure 3. Information Needs Matrix.

Information Literacy

As the form and use of information changes, so do the perimeters of information literacy. Before we examine information literacy perhaps we should examine a number of questions for the workplace. The answers to these questions will differ in each environment.

- What information does the enterprise need?
  - What is the source, scope, level and content of this information.
  - What format will be most useful?
  - What other sources need to be related to this information?
- Who needs the information?
  - What skills or knowledge or cognitive power do they need to use this information effectively?
- What tasks does the information need to support?
- Are there related tasks which require similar information?

We might call this an "Information Needs Assessment." This type of information needs assessment must be examined from many perspectives including:

1. The enterprise
2. The person
3. The tasks to be performed

Figure 3 is a beginning of a matrix for considering the topics an enterprise might look at as factors affecting its information needs based upon the person or the information user's characteristics and the tasks being performed.

Making Information Available Is Not Enough

Just making the information available is not enough. But, making information more useful is key. Personalized attention, training and after service responsiveness are now competitive requirements. This will become even more important in the future. Which technologies are changing the nature of work? What are their implications to the work environment? How will you (the information professional) manage and distribute this information? How will you train the users? What follow up services need your support? What value will you add to the information or the process?

What do tools for enterprise and data analysis, repository management, multimedia interfaces, expert systems and executive information systems offer? How will they aid the information process? What jobs will these changes create? How do we plan for the information needs of these yet to be defined jobs?

New information appliances are emerging and changing the way people relate to information. "High tech/high touch" has come to mean the new relationship between people and technology. Now users have rapid access to information, procedures and tools which will transform the way people work. It will require people to do new jobs. From this point of view, the computer should not be seen as just a machine to execute tasks, but as an ever present personal tutor which allows the user to begin learning at their own pace. The same information and communication technologies which are so rapidly transforming our world can provide just-in-time training to meet these challenges of change.

Today, a growing number of firms are relying on interactive multimedia to handle many of the teaching tasks previously reserved for individual trainers. Not only is this approach used to teach people how to use computers and the associated software, but increasingly specific job related skills. Firms can significantly decrease their training expenses and increase their return-on-investment for training by reducing the learning time, hours spent in a classroom, travel time and expenses, time away from the job for training.

As was suggested earlier with the introduction of new banking technology (HPTS), the multimedia solution approach offers the capabilities of realism and interactivity. With multimedia, life-like images and sound can be used in a multi-sensory approach to learning.

The integration of information and communication technologies provide additional enhancement to the personal computer as a personal tutor. For example, recently IBM announced a new adapter card which supports a wide range of full-motion, color video and stereo sound capabilities. This new technology allows standard Personal System/2 color monitors to support full motion, windowed video.

CD-ROM (Compact Disc Read Only Memory), the same technology that revitalized the music industry is now being used to store, access and distribute information. Application programs and data bases can be distributed along with installation procedures on the same media. CD-ROM provides a durable and highly reliable medium compared with diskettes, according to Gary Barron with IBM's Customer Application Center in Atlanta.

Another recent offering uses hypertext linking techniques and digitized, high quality audio (between AM and FM level) and photo-like color images. The "Audio Video Connection" uses sound, display, and motion effects to provide an eye-catching, fast paced, and attention-holding way to communicate information.

An easy-to-use and inexpensive authoring system for the novice developer to tap with the power of the personal computer called "LinkWay" was recently announced for the IBM Personal System/2. Now, teachers can assemble educational modules or entire classes that use graphics, motion and sound.

There are many opportunities to explore when you begin to look at the personal computer as a personal tutor. For example, approximately six hundred interactive education and instructional courseware products produced by many different vendors are listed in the IBM MultiMedia Solutions catalog.

Information Literacy: The Future Is Now

As we have discussed today, information literacy is a very complex topic with many attributes to consider. We all recognize that demographics, economics, technologies, and even industry orientations are shifting. We know that information can help us to identify market niches, make our employees more knowledgeable and productive, develop competitive advantages, have the right capabilities and cost structures and achieve better implementations of results. We have heard that even the performance expectation for employees will require more sophisticated job skills, training and information knowledge.

We know that making information available is not enough. We can see that using communication and information technologies to make people more information literate is a viable approach. There are many choices.

We need to consider the changes taking place. We need to understand the impacts of the changes on our profession, enterprises, and employees. We need to think, analyze and plan for the future. Today, I have offered you lots of questions and very few answers. As I mentioned earlier, thirty minutes is not enough time to answer such complex questions. Besides, I don't have all the answers even if you gave me all week to talk. I do hope, though, that you have gained some insights into the challenges we face in helping workers to be information literate and more productive in the work place of tomorrow.

Bibliography

Ames, Charles B., and James D. Hlavacek. *Market Driven Management*. Homewood, IL: Dow-Jones-Irwin, 1989.

Farrell, Kathy, and Craig Broude. *Winning the Change Game: How to Implement Information Systems with Fewer Headaches and Bigger Paybacks*. Los Angeles: Breakthroughs Enterprises, 1987.

Gery, Gloria. *Making CBT Happen: Prescriptions for Successful Implementation of Computer-Based Training in Your Organization*. Boston: Weingarten Publications, 1987.

Goldstein, Irwin L., and associates. *Training and Development in Organizations*. San Francisco: Jossey-Bass, 1989.

IBM Corporation Publications: ImagePlus High Performance Transaction System General Information Manual GC31-2706-0; Info-Window System G580−0852-00; MultiMedia Courseware Catalog G580-0845-02; MultiMedia Solutions in Higher Education GK20-2262; The Action Media (tm) 750 Delivery and Capture Adapters; The M-Motion Video Adapter/A G221-2925-00. Atlanta: IBM Corporation MultiMedia Solutions, 1989, 1990.

Kraemer, Kenneth L.; John Leslie King; Debora E. Dunkle; and Joseph P. Lane. *Managing Information Systems: Change and Control in Organizational Computing.* San Francisco: Jossey-Bass, 1989.

London, Manuel. *Managing the Training Enterprises: High-Quality, Cost-Effective Employee Training in Organizations.* San Francisco: Jossey-Bass, 1989.

————. *Managing Beyond the Quick Fix.* San Francisco: Jossey-Bass, 1989.

Naisbitt, John. *Megatrends.* New York: Warner, 1982.

————, and Patricia Aburdene. *Megatrends 2000.* New York: William Morrow, 1990.

Pinchot, Gifford, III. *Intrapreneuring: Why You Don't Have to Leave the Corporation to Become an Entrepreneur.* New York: Harper and Row, 1985.

Porter, Michael E. *Competitive Advantage: Creating and Sustaining Superior Performance.* New York: Free Press, 1985.

Quinn, Karen Takle. "The Information Center—Another Perspective." *Online* 6 (July 1982): 11-23.

————. "Libraries Are Lifelong Learning Centers." In *ASEE Annual Conference Proceedings, 1978* (Career Management Lifelong Learning), pp. 292-94. Washington, DC: American Society for Engineering Education, 1978.

————, ed. *Advances in Office Automation.* New York: Wiley, 1985.

Rice, Ronald E. and associates. *The New Media: Communication, Research, and Technology.* Beverly Hills, CA: Sage, 1984.

Strassman, Paul A. *Information Payoff: The Transformation of Work in the Electronic Age.* New York: Free Press, 1985.

Synnott, William R. *The Information Weapon: Winning Customers and Markets with Technology.* New York: Wiley, 1987.

Taylor, Bruce A. "An Agent for Education Change." *Human Capital* 1 (April 1990): 24-27.

Vobejda, B. "New Mazda Plant in Michigan." *Washington Post,* 14 April 1987.

Redesigning Access:
What We Must Do to Help
Information Seekers Succeed in
the Electronic Environment

Prudence Ward Dalrymple

My interest in redesigning access stems from a concern with helping users to become more successful in their quest for information. When Pat Schuman spoke about users and nonusers, I realized that in my prepared remarks, I had only the term users, but I want to be sure that you understand that I am talking about nonusers as well, and perhaps particularly about nonusers. I am talking about people in general, not just that fraction of the population that we know as library users.

I would also like to follow up on what Karen Takle Quinn said about her information literacy requirements matrix that lays out personality and task characteristics in relation to enterprise factors. I was very interested and pleased to see the middle column that emphasizes the affect, or the motive aspect. I think that that is something we don't pay a lot of attention to in libraries. It is a growing area of concern, and one that interests me a great deal.

I would like to sketch out the parameters of the problems I see regarding users' performance in the emerging electronic library. Helping users is an enormous problem in our profession. It is one of the central problems in our field today, and it deserves the attention of some of our most able and creative minds. But because it's such a large and complex problem, I'd like to begin by outlining the domain of the issue, as I see it, and by offering some definitions. In that way, we can travel through some of these complex thickets without losing our way, or each other. I will then summarize some research findings about users' behavior, and mention some of the work that has been done to enhance information retrieval systems. Finally, I will suggest further directions for research and development in this field.

I. The Domain: The Electronic Environment

We have all heard of the electronic environment, and most of us are familiar with the notion of the library without walls. This "new" library is best described as a function, not a location; as a process, not a place. This new library is not ubiquitous, however. Rather, it is slowly heaving into existence, mostly on college campuses in large public library systems, and sometimes in corporate settings. Visions of the scholar's workstation, the executive's information system, which we have seen this afternoon, or the family who uses its television to locate the latest materials on toxic waste, bran muffins or on genetically transformed adolescent turtles are, for the most part, still visions, and not realities.

Yet the technology is here to support these visions, and librarians are well advised, but perhaps ill-equipped, to take a proactive role in shaping these changes. These technologies are based on digital information systems—the machine readable records that comprise the online catalogs, the CD-ROMs, and the databases that all of us know so well. Right now these technologies are bounded both physically and temporally, at specific locations and during limited time periods. What will change in the electronic "library without walls" is that these same technologies, or very similar ones, will be available from any terminal, or microcomputer or television, and at virtually any time of day or night. The telecommunications links are already in place, ready to hook up all of these technologies into vast information networks. For example, it is possible to search from a single terminal in the Midwest, right in my office, the online catalogs at UCLA, Dartmouth, and the University of Michigan. Where these catalogs also include databases such a PsychINFO (the online version of *Psychological Abstracts*), the user can search these resources as well. The familiar CD-ROM workstation, dedicated to a single information resource such as ERIC, or InfoTRac, and so on, can be linked to several other databases in local area networks, and more importantly, this technology (optical laser disk technology) is being incorporated into workstations such as the NeXT workstation designed by Steve Jobs (formerly of Apple) and numerous other examples, as Karen Takle Quinn has pointed out. For my purpose here, what is most important about these technologies is that they have the following two properties:

1. **They are available for free.** The sponsoring agency (the library, the campus, etc.) pays for them up front, and makes them available to a particular constituency free of charge. There is no "use charge" and therefore, use is encouraged in order to justify the considerable initial investment.

2. **They are designed to be searched directly by users, not by librarians.** There are other properties of these systems, such as their fluidity, their ability to be captured in whole or in part and then manipulated, and their dependence on the inverted file structure—but I am not concerned with these properties in this discussion.

So, in summary, I am concerned with electronic information sources such as online catalogs, CD-ROMs, and locally mounted databases that are designed to be searched directly by the end-user. I am not concerned with fee-based searches of systems such as BRS or DIALOG conducted by librarians trained as search analysts; not that I don't think that that's important, but that's not my concern today.

Before turning to what we know about the end-users and their searching performance, I'd like to take a closer look at the components of these systems themselves, just so that we are clear as to what we are talking about, and that we share a common vocabulary and understanding of the system parts.

II. The Information Systems Themselves

Information systems of the type we are concerned with consist of the following parts:

a. **The database.** This comprises the actual machine-readable records and indexes themselves. In an OPAC (online public access catalog) this is the MARC record. In a database or CD-ROM, it is the bibliographic record consisting of fields such as the author, title, journal, abstract, descriptors, and so on. It also contains the indexes to these fields.

b. **The searching language.** The most common way of referring to the search language is by describing it as the "command language" or the "command mode." This is usually meant to contrast it with "menu mode" or "natural language"; "natural language" being the way we speak, not the way we typically search.

c. **The search engine.** In most systems, this means the way in which the command structure and the database architecture interact to process a search. In most systems this consists of inverted word and phrase indexes that support access by both keyword and controlled vocabulary (subject headings and descriptors), the use of Boolean and proximity operators, and the processing of a search statement, character by character, to produce an "exact match" between the command and the retrieved set.

d. **The interface.** In my opinion, interface is the dirtiest word in the information retrieval industry today. It is over-used and abused. It can cover almost anything across the board. It's an area where a great deal of improvement has occurred — a lot of bells and whistles have been added in the interface. Unfortunately, we don't always understand what people mean when they talk about the interface. It can include things like screen displays, help screens, error messages and diagnostics, levels of access such as novice access or expert access mode, and various "intelligent" features such as automatic truncation, online thesauri, automatic supply of Boolean operators, and post-processing such as display of the output.

e. **External enhancements.** I have coined a new term, "external enhancements," that is my catch-all term for anything that exists from outside of the information system itself. Examples would be automatic dialing into external databases, provision of space to save searches or catches, or tutorials that are designed to assist users in learning how to search.

I think it will be helpful to keep these components in mind as we discuss problems that users have in searching for information in the electronic environment, and particularly as we consider what has been done and what can be done to ensure that users have a successful experience. As I have said before most of the work that has been done on system design has been at the interface and at the external enhancement level. Very little work has been done at the database level where the actual records are concerned, partly because that's such an enormous task, when you think about all the MARC records that exist in the world or all of the bibliographic records that exist in a system such as DIALOG. There has been a little work done on search engines, in looking at things like probabilistic retrieval and display of relevancy or display of citations by possible relevancy.

III. What Do We Know About Users and Their Problems in Accessing Electronic Information Sources?

Most of the research that I will try to summarize comes from people in the academic environment, but a good deal of it also comes from library practitioners. I want to make a special point of that—that research is not limited just to those of us who are in academe—that there is a lot of good work that is being done out in the field. I would like to see even more of that done, possibly in conjunction with academics. The people out on the front line have a wonderful opportunity to provide really helpful and very insightful data as to what's really going on with users in the library. The names are probably familiar to many, if not most of you: Christine Borgman, Karen Markey, Brian Nielsen and Betsy Baker, Marcia Bates, Nicholas Belkin, and Charles Hildreth.[1]

In my summary of research findings, I have broken things into two major groups. The first group is what I call external observations about the process; the second group is called the internal process of searching. These are very rough categories, but they help to keep things straight. I'll cover each of these points and then go back and elaborate a little bit more.

1. The first one is that most users want what we call "one-stop shopping." That is, they want to be able to access books, periodicals, and other information resources from one single access point.

2. Most users, fortunately or unfortunately, don't read documentation or manuals. Most of them don't attend training sessions or don't have them available to them, and they don't consult thesauri or subject heading lists—either printed or online.

3. Most users who search electronic databases "like" to do so, and report high levels of "satisfaction," whatever that means. We have a huge area of very general terms such as "like" and "satisfaction" that really need to be parsed out and explored at a more detailed level.

4. Subject searching, that is, topical searches, are the most common kind of search in an electronic environment.

5. Selecting an appropriate database is a concept that most users have never been confronted with: when they are, such as in choosing a CD-ROM workstation, they choose correctly only about a quarter of the time.

6. In the second group of findings, the ones that relate more to the internal process of searching, most users, even experienced users, do not exploit all the system capabilities that are available to them.

7. In online catalogs, particularly when keyword access is not available, over a third of searches result in nothing retrieved, and where keyword access is available in a database, users often retrieve large sets, and have difficulty refining their output. So we see two ends of the spectrum — caught between a rock and a hard place — either nothing or too much.

8. Users have difficulty formulating a search statement initially, and tend not to be able to develop a strategy that entails more than one or two steps. Users also have difficulty changing or modifying their search.

I think most librarians recognize that the results achieved by users are smaller, and less "precise" than the results achieved by search intermediaries. This has led to concern on the part of librarians as to the quality and quantity of information identified by users who are searching on their own. Questions such as, "Are users finding all that's available on the topic?" "Are they finding the best/newest materials on a topic?" "Are users finding enough?" are on the lips of many librarians, particularly those who are actively participating in the arena of end-user searching. Many of you who work in undergraduate libraries or in public libraries, have articulated those concerns, either to yourself or to your colleagues.

I'd like to go back through each one of these steps and expand on these findings and share with you a few thoughts about what can be done or has been done to address these problems.

IV. What We Are Doing to Enhance Users' Success

1. **Most users want one-stop shopping.** This desire translates into a number of innovations introduced into systems. The "supercatalog" that was described at a discussion forum at the ALA Midwinter meeting in January 1990 mentioned the inclusion of periodical databases with the online catalog. Whenever this issue is mentioned, I am reminded of an incident that occurred while I was visiting a friend in

Washington, D.C., several years ago. I became engaged in a conversation with my cab driver, who turned out to be a graduate student who was moonlighting. When he learned that I was a librarian, he proceeded to harangue me about the limitations of library systems, including the fact that we librarians seemed unwilling or unable to provide journal literature along with book materials with a single search. Little did he know of the technical problems associated with accommodating his desire! Nonetheless, it was a legitimate goal, and with the supercatalog, one step has been taken toward achieving that objective. On the other hand I would like to suggest that the "supercatalog" concept remains firmly grounded in librarians' perceptions of information. It retains all the trappings of bibliographic control and format, rather than being grounded in the perceptions of the user. One colleague of mine fondly refers to the on-line catalog as the card catalog on wheels. We really haven't changed things all that much; we just repackaged it for our convenience so that we can update without having to change all those cards. A "better" approach is the concept of a scholar's workstation which examines the work habits of scholars (or executives, or whoever) to determine what resources are required, in what format, and through what access points. It is this notion of beginning with the user that I believe is an absolutely essential premise of designing effective systems for users. It is a reversal (I hope) of the truism that libraries are designed for librarians, not for users. It can also provide a platform for librarians to act as user advocates when dealing with vendors and other system designers outside the library profession.

2. **Most users do not read documentation or manuals, don't attend training sessions, and do not consult thesauri or subject heading lists, either in print or online.** Most users prefer to receive their help or coaching in an informal, one-to-one mode. Since this is both time-consuming and labor-intensive, it is only rarely able to be offered. Instead, help screens, and hypermedia-like supports are increasingly being built into systems. The diagnostic capabilities that use artificial intelligence to recognize where users are having difficulty are a very sophisticated form of online help. The design of these facilities, and it is a major effort, is often a team effort drawing on the skills of educational psychologists, librarians, and computer scientists. We will see even more developments in these areas in the future.

I recently attended a conference on expert systems and artificial intelligence (AI) held at the University of Illinois, and that gave me an insight into what's being done. There are barriers to achieving what we would like to see, but certainly there are a lot of people with very good minds who are tending to this issue of providing AI and expert systems in the library.

3. Subject searching is the most common kind of search in an electronic environment. By subject searching here I want to draw a distinction that I discovered is important to make. When I gave a presentation at ALA in New Orleans, I was talking about subject searching and realized in the question and answer period that what I was describing as subject searching—meaning topical search, coming from my background as a special librarian in health science—was being interpreted by my largely technical systems, or cataloguing audience as being a search on a subject heading, and nothing could be further from the truth. I as speaker and they as audience were just completely counter to each other in terms of what we really meant. So I have revised my talks to say topical searches not subject searches.

Users generally don't use subject headings and probably most of you know that. Searching capabilities that were previously available only to trained search analysts working with large bibliographic systems are now available in online catalogs and CD-ROMs, primarily through keyboard access, giving expanded searching powers to even the most unsophisticated user, which is both good and bad. Along with expanded searching powers has come a bewildering multiplicity of system features and interface characteristics. Loading the Dewey classification system along with the online catalog, for example, was tried in one experimental study. The conversion of some indexes from magnetic tape to optical disc storage has prompted some producers to redesign the database and to introduce a variety of innovations including loading thesauri such as MeSH (medical subject headings), or providing a hypertext-like function in order to navigate through a citation database. This is exemplified in the CD-ROM versions of *Science Citation Index,* and several CD-ROM versions of MEDLINE, ERIC, and PsychINFO. If any of you have looked at the CD-ROM version of *Science Citation Index* you will recognize that it bears very little resemblance to what we are familiar with in online versions of that database.

4. Selecting an appropriate database is a concept that most users have never been confronted with. They've never had the opportunities to select, so that they've never been confronted with that challenge. The proliferation of information retrieval systems in many libraries, particularly academic libraries, has bewildered many an unwary user, particularly the undergraduate. Confusion about systems is not unusual; but what is more worrisome is when users seem to be unaware that alternatives exist when they have no idea where they are searching. I offer an extreme example, one that is not even associated with the electronic library, coming from my own research, in which one subject in an experiment conducted all of his topical searches (subject searches), in the author/title divided catalog.[2] The research assistant who was observing the search commented when he came back to my office — "He didn't deserve to find anything — but he did!" While this is offered as an example of an incorrect source selection, I am reminded that as librarians we often make assumptions about the ways in which people search for information — that people who are searching by author or title are looking for a "known item" rather than for topical information. But, on the other hand, how many times do we, ourselves, look for materials on a given topic by looking under an author's name who is known to have written on that subject, particularly when the terminology or subject headings with which to express that topic escapes us.

In a study conducted at the University of Illinois just last year only about a quarter of the students who were using CD-ROMs at the undergraduate library were using the appropriate system.[3] The database selection features such as those developed by DIALOG and BRS are basic necessities for effective searching in the electronic environment, but how they are designed, and how they are explained to the user remains to be determined. And I must say that those systems, whereas they are very helpful, are certainly primitive and we have really not explored the whole issue of source selection in an electronic environment.

5. **Boolean logic is confusing to most users.** Many studies have shown that users have difficulty understanding and using Boolean operators correctly. For example, most users inadvertently over-restrict their search statements by adding more and more terms and linking them with the operator "AND." This is particularly problematic when the additional terms are similar or even synonymous. For example, a search statement such as: "online searching *and* database searching in college *and* university libraries" is likely to result in a null set, retrieving nothing and leading the user to conclude that "the library just doesn't have anything on my topic." In another example taken from my own research, we found that of twenty subjects asked to search for materials in a university online catalog, only one person used Boolean operators at all — and he was an engineering student! Yet Boolean operators are one of the first features that most librarians, when asked, will say must be present in a particular system. I'm not say-

ing that they shouldn't be, but we may have to massage them a great deal before they become effective for our users. One of the ways these have been massaged in some systems is by automatically supplying the Boolean operator "OR" as people are entering search terms or words because it is felt that left to their own devices, people will use the operator "AND" and so "OR" is provided the appropriate operator.

As I mentioned before, these above five areas are what I regard as being the internal, more psychological aspects of searching that I find particularly fascinating. I see the library and particularly on-line or electronic libraries as being a wonderful laboratory for us in the library field and also in allied fields such as psychology to learn about the cognitive process of information seeking.

6. **Most users, even experienced users, do not exploit all the system capabilities available to them.** The history of online searching is replete with reports that even experienced searchers conduct fairly simple searches in bibliographic databases. While studies of experienced librarians searching online catalogs are few and far between, we have little reason to suspect that in subject searching at least, most librarians will perform any differently than our users. Such a finding may lead us to suggest that either our eyes are bigger than our stomachs when it comes to features within a system — we want more system capabilities than we really need — or that we have failed to specify correctly what capabilities are most desirable.

The difference between experienced searchers and novices is one area in which we can make interventions. Some systems provide at least two modes of searching. DIALOG, for example, offers both a menu-driven and a command-mode approach to its CD-ROM products. Users are free to select whichever mode they prefer. A recent announcement from DIALOG suggests that these two modes, which up until now have been kept separate, will be able to interact with each other so that users who are attempting to use the command mode and who get stuck may switch into the menu mode to complete their search. The user can also ask for a display of the search strategy as it would have appeared in the command mode for purposes of comparison, and one hopes, for purposes of instruction as well. To what extent this capability will be exploited, and what effect it will have on users' ability to construct more effective searches, however, remains to be seen.

The ability to customize a system to its users is an idea that has grown out of the concept of user modeling. Through the use of artificial intelligence, systems can be "taught" to "remember" certain things about the user so that preferences for certain output formats, particular search strategies, search parameters and the like can be invoked automatically when the searcher logs onto the system. Presumably, these features can be added gradually, so that eventually the information retrieval system can be as customized as many PC's are now. Those of you who have to share a PC with other people in your library or office often may recognize that people go in and do something to the system and customize it in a way that, if they don't tell you what they have done, it can be really confusing. But there is evidence that people do like to put their own mark on an otherwise anonymous system.

7. **In online catalogs, particularly when keyword access is not available, over a third of searches result in nothing retrieved. When keyword access is available, users often retrieve large sets, and have difficulty refining their output.** One of the most problematic areas in information retrieval is vocabulary. Librarians have committed enormous resources to the maintenance of controlled vocabulary and subject authority control, concepts that escape most users. There are a variety of factors that contribute to this situation, a situation that I see as a major failure in communication between librarians and our constituents. The gap between the terms used in subject headings and those used by searchers is all too familiar to those of us who keep up with the literature (e.g. Sanford Berman and people who would like to revise the Library of Congress Subject Headings). Yet most librarians defend the value of controlled vocabulary, and are committed to its maintenance. Because this is the case, the problem then becomes one of mapping users into the vocabulary of the systems. A variety of solutions have been proposed to this problem over the past twenty years, but none has been implemented to date. Research in what is known as natural language processing is ongoing, but there are very few people capable of conducting that research and progress is therefore quite slow.

Despite the fact that authority control is often regarded as a service to users — co-locating and bringing together all of the materials on a particular topic — users have little or no input into the construction of thesauri, or subject heading lists. Yet, involving users in the creation and maintenance of searching vocabularies was proposed nearly thirty years ago and continues to be proposed today and in some cases is being implemented on a very small scale. For example, in an experimental interface at the University of Illinois, users may propose additional terms for the controlled vocabulary; these are reviewed by librarians and considered for permanent inclusion in its local database system.[4]

The personal HYPERCATalog project that was initiated at LIBLAB at Linköping University in Sweden also has features whereby authors and users can indicate preferred indexing terms and they can leave a "usage trail" through the catalog which subsequent searchers may follow.[5] The image that I always have when I think about that is of a large meadow where perhaps a deer or hikers have gone across the meadow and eventually they have gone across the meadow on the same pathway long enough so that they leave a trail. It's interesting to watch people's behavior: even if the trail is not a straight line, the most direct way from point A to point B, people will tend to follow that trail, because it's there. I think we might see that in large databases such as catalogs eventually.

8. **Users have difficulty formulating a search statement initially, and tend not to be able to develop a strategy that entails more than one or two steps.** One of the greatest benefits of electronic information retrieval is its interactivity. The ability to move through "information space," once acquired, is an important skill for survival in the information-rich electronic environment. Yet two of the barriers to acquiring this skill are, as I see it, the "blank screen" and the ability to "converse" or to dialog with the system effectively. The effect of both of these barriers can be lessened by what I call feedback. In my own work, I have suggested that the kind and degree of feedback in a system will affect users' ability to find what they want, and will affect their attitudes about their results and about the system. And you remember I mentioned Karen Takle Quinn's remarks about the inclusion in her matrix of the affect — of the emotional aspects of interaction with technology. Feedback will also help people move forward toward achieving a goal in their information search. These ideas are not unique to me, but derive from work in cognitive science which itself is an interdisciplinary field encompassing psychology, philosophy, linguistics, and computer science, all of which are cognate fields to the field of library and information studies.

More specifically, the blank screen, or the null set, gives no feedback to the user. The designers of the Macintosh interface recognized this, and nowhere are you confronted with the blinking cursor as you were in the early days of DOS-based systems, before IBM learned from Apple (Karen reminds me this really came from Xerox, and she's right). Similarly, the ready availability of "helpful suggestions" as to how to exploit the feedback that is already extant in the system, such as lists of descriptors or subject headings applied to a bibliographic record, can assist a user in navigating through information space. The importance of context in moving through an information space is easily admitted; this idea is reflected in the psychological theory of human memory that provided the theoretical framework for my initial research into user searching models. This theory, called "Retrieval by Reformulation," suggests that the process of refinement, or changing direction, and reformulating a search is a process that comes very naturally to human beings—we do it all the time ourselves when we "wrack our brains" or "search our memories" for a bit of information. I'd like to just give you a classic example. If somebody asks you how many windows were there on the north side of the house in which you grew up, most of us cannot retrieve that bit of information instantaneously. But if we close our eyes, and imagine ourselves in our childhood home, and orient ourselves to the points of the compass, we can walk through room by room and answer that question. So, it is by creating a context and moving through that that we begin to gain access to a wealth of information. The ability to design that context into an information system will enable people to draw upon that and evoke it immediately without it always having to be in place. There is a lot of very technical computerese that I don't understand about being able to evoke or instantiate a particular system at the time that it's needed rather than having to have it in place in a static form all the time. The process of association, or finding a context, is well-known to those who study memory processes. When these ideas are translated into information retrieval systems, the process of searching will become far more naturalistic for users.

V. Future Directions to Enhancing End-User Searching

So where do we go from here? For the last several years, librarians have taken two essentially different approaches to the problems of end-user searching: the bibliographic instruction approach and the system design approach. Carol Kuhlthau talked a lot about bibliographic instruction and my domain is the system design approach, but I'd like to propose that we can perhaps integrate these approaches. Before I do that, I'd like to offer a few comments about some of the problems that are limitations to bibliographic instruction as I see them. Last year at the ALA annual meeting in Dallas, the Association of College and Research Libraries, Bibliographic Instruction Section sponsored its second "Think Tank" on bibliographic instruction, and during the last two years we have witnessed major efforts directed at information literacy—this afternoon's colloquium being a good example. I would like to reiterate the definition of information literacy suggested by Hannelore Rader and Bill Coons in their position paper that was prepared for the Think Tank. They defined information literacy as the ability to effectively access and evaluate information for problem solving and decision making. In this context, achieving information literacy is a broad-based, labor-intensive activity that may extend across a lifetime and encompass a variety of resources beyond the library and librarians. Unfortunately much of the effort that could be directed toward information literacy skills in libraries is now being directed toward troubleshooting and bootstrapping operations in order to overcome or compensate for the problems that users have in accessing the information systems already in place. Thus I am suggesting that a very first step in achieving information literacy is through system design.

There are several reasons for this. Not surprisingly, the first one is economic. Bibliographic instruction—even minimal instruction—is expensive. It "uses up" our librarians, and our support staff. It is available only during certain hours. Because of the variety of information systems in any given individual's world, the "how to" of access must be learned and re-learned each time a new system is encountered. BI is inefficient—most users prefer to be coached one-on-one; aside from the intrinsic satisfaction that many of us who have worked in reference capacities, we know that it is very satisfying to coach a user so that they have an "Aha" experience, and finally see the light on how to gain access to information. But most of us don't have that opportunity all the time and we are often reduced to giving answers to directional questions and repeating the same set of instructions over and over again. Bibliographic instruction is most appropriate in an academic environment—a school, college, or university. Many users do not have the opportunity to be in such an environment, nor do they see it as appropriate. Our time in the academic environment for most of us is limited—we don't spend our entire lives in the classroom. So, "traditional" BI is restricted both to a particular time and a particular place in most of our lives.

I don't want to create the impression that I am against bibliographic instruction or that the goals of BI are not worthwhile. Quite the contrary, and I'd like to relate a recent incident to support that. I attended a conference last weekend on teaching in higher education in which one of the speakers made the following points. He described the changing role of the professor, beginning with the aesthetic "man/woman of culture" of the late nineteenth and early twentieth centuries, and then went on to describe the "technical expert" of the post-war years, to the "teacher as radical or guru" model of the counterculture. He suggested that the challenge for today's (and tomorrow's) world should be to cultivate critical intelligence and civic responsibility, in other words, information literacy; to reinstate values and goals back into the university; and to work with others toward the common good of society. In arriving at this conclusion, he drew upon an early model of medical practice, dating from ancient Greece. As a medical librarian I sat up and paid particular attention to this. In classical times, there was a two-tiered system of medical practice. The practitioners known as the empiricists dispensed therapies — medication and other treatments — to their patients, while the other group, the scientific medical practitioners, taught their patients how to become well and how to stay healthy. And I think it's this last model that we would strive for in librarianship.

While I am not sure that the history of librarianship necessarily parallels that of higher education — and I particularly question whether librarians have ever been regarded as "gurus" — I do think there are some useful parallels. We have moved from seeing the library as the temple of culture to a point where we see librarians as technical experts, sometimes given to jumping on the latest technological bandwagon. So, small wonder that the values represented by bibliographic instruction and information literacy have been welcomed by many of us who are tired of being intimidated by computerese.

But just as higher education faces a dilemma in determining how to teach classes of three to four hundred undergraduates — how to do that without "burning out" our faculty — librarians face a similar dilemma in how we can provide the information literacy skills to our students without "burning out" our reference librarians. We simply don't have the money or the resources to engage in the individualized assistance we would like to give. Just as universities have been forced to utilize teaching assistants in large classes, we have used paraprofessionals at the reference desk. But just as those in higher education are exploring ways to incorporate new technologies into teaching, in libraries we have the opportunity to take an active role in designing systems that can instruct and encourage users, while at the same time perform information retrieval functions. Meeting this challenge will not be easy, but we have taken some steps already which I have described. And I would like to propose a model in which we can make some forward movement toward creating an environment where users can be successful in searching for information in the electronic environment.

VI. Conclusion

In a paper recently submitted for publication, a colleague and I have proposed that the approaches taken in bibliographic instruction and system design be grouped together and called "informed retrieval."[6] We define informed retrieval as using the feedback from an information system in order to improve retrieval results. The feedback is provided by the system and is integral to the system design. It is under the control of the user, however, and can be evoked as needed. Informed retrieval places control squarely in the hands of the user, thus empowering him or her with the same abilities as the skilled indexer.

Tangential to this model, I would like to mention that my co-author on this paper is a woman who has spent her entire life in technical services and in cataloguing. I spent my entire professional life in information services and in reference. In our conversations over the years, we recognized that the divisions that exist in our field, even in some of our library school curricula, between public services and technical services have really been counterproductive. We see informed retrieval as beginning to take system design—the database design that's dependent upon the records themselves—and integrating that with the needs of the user, and thus diminishing or blurring those boundaries that are basically administrative boundaries that reflect the way our libraries are organized, rather than the way users seek information.

A key feature of informed retrieval provides feedback during the search process, notifying searchers of their location in the database relative to its structure, and of their progress in locating relevant materials. In other words, the system provides feedback as to where the searcher is located in the search, whether there is more information available, and what can be done to retrieve it. Some of the features described earlier are examples of informed retrieval, such as interventions that display descriptors and ask whether the user wishes to see other documents indexed to these terms, and systems that display graphically (or otherwise) indications of the probable relevancy of documents within a set. Still other systems supply automatic truncation or "wild card" features to increase retrieval, although unless the system informs the user of what it's doing or that such a feature has been invoked, confusion often results and the system fails to truly "inform" the searching process. As mentioned earlier, users themselves often customize an information retrieval system by creating commonly-needed search strategies as "macros" or "hedges" and storing them at the searching station and invoking them as needed.

While the premises on which these ideas are based are not new, they are much closer to widespread implementation because the technology is now available to support them. Our increased understanding of user behavior drawn from cognitive science and psychology, enables us to specify more accurately which features are most likely to be effective. It is this combination of understanding the user, not just as a library user, but as a human being engaged in the process of seeking information in the electronic environment, that will give us direction and insight into designing systems to help users succeed in the electronic environment. So as I conclude, I would like to reiterate that it is this focus on users and their information seeking situations that will enable us to design systems for users, and maybe eventually systems for nonusers, not just for librarians.

References

1. For those interested in delving more deeply into the subject, two excellent starting points are Christine Borgman's "Why Are Online Catalogs Hard to Use? Lessons Learned from Information-Retrieval Studies," *Journal of the American Society for Information Science* 37 (November 1986): 387–400, and William H. Mischo and Jounghyoun Lee, "End-User Searching of Bibliographic Databases," *Annual Review of Information Science* vol. 22, pp. 227–63 (Elsevier, 1987).

2. Prudence W. Dalrymple, "Retrieval by Reformulation in Two Library Catalogs: Toward a Cognitive Model for Searching Behavior," *Journal of the American Society for Information Science* 41 (June 1990): 272–81.

3. Gillian Allen, "Database Selection by Patrons Using CD-ROM," *College and Research Libraries* 51 (January 1990): 69–75.

4. William Mischo et al., "The University of Illinois at Urbana-Champaign," in *Campus Strategies for Libraries and Electronic Information,* ed. by Caroline Arms (Bedford, MA: Digital Press, 1990), pp. 117–41.

5. Roland Hjerppe, "Hypercat at LIBLAB in Sweden," in *The On-Line Catalog: Developments and Directions,* ed. by Charles R. Hildreth (London: The Library Association, 1989), pp. 177–209.

6. Prudence W. Dalrymple and Jennifer A. Younger, "From Authority Control to Informed Retrieval: Framing the Expanded Domain of Subject Access," *College & Research Libraries* 52 (March 1991): 139–49.

Dealing with User Behavior: A Prerequisite for Librarian Involvement in the Information Literacy Movement

Charles Curran

I saw this in a *New Yorker* cartoon.

Once, about twenty years ago, at the checkout counter of the Piggly Wiggly shortly after the surgeon general had ordered a warning to appear on all cigarette packs, a man reached for a single package of cigarettes. "Harry, don't take those cigarettes," ordered his companion, his wife, I believe. "They don't have the warning on them. They aren't fresh!"

I relate that episode because I believe it captures in allegory the core of the message I will report today. *Whatever plans we have for doing good, for spreading the word, for providing access to technologically enhanced information retrieval processes, these plans better include a consideration for users and their behavior.*

These plans had better include a consideration for users and their behavior. Harry and his wife were not illiterate. Harry and his wife were not *information* illiterate. Nor were they non-users of information. But their behavior is a product of their socio-economic status and their value systems. I believe that all of us who champion the cause of literacy, cultural literacy, computer literacy and information literacy must consider the reality that only those activities and pursuits which fit the user's value system are likely to appeal to him or her. What that means is: we can not expect people to behave the way we would like them to simply by pointing out to them that what we have would make their lives better.

Perhaps this meaning can be usefully explored if we focus upon this idea of behavior and then define what is meant by information literacy.

Understanding how people can get at the information they need or want requires us to observe the behavior of information itself.

First it comes into being. Then it travels. It begets more information. It explodes. It proliferates. It pollutes. And as it does all these things, information assumes a variety of forms: oral, print, non-print and electronic.

In addition to this behavior, it has some related properties.

First of all, information is not *used up* when *used*. A good novel read by one person is also read by another and another. This can not be said for other commodities which are gone once they are used. Take a Big Mac, for example.

Secondly, good information confers *power* upon the consumer and the organization or person who provides it. Bad information, on the other hand, and information which nobody wants, confers *un-power*.

Thirdly, even good information can become obsolete in the blink of an eye.

Understanding how people can get information they want or need also requires us to observe the behavior of people *toward* that information and its flow.

> They use it.
> They misuse it.
> They ignore it.

Well, they do use it and many of our information places are bursting at the seams, both with information and with users of information. We use information we get from our family and friends so often, the phenomenon earned the name: backfence college. Highly educated users of highly specialized information rely so often upon their own and their colleagues files, we had to give that a name too: invisible college. The information seeking in the backfence colleges and the invisible colleges — members of which may be voracious consumers of information — can exist in near total isolation from our libraries and information centers.

They misuse it too. Harry and his wife did. Inside traders do. The legion of decency used to condemn movies. They created a virtual desiderata — a want list for curious movie goers.

Again, I would like to suggest for our consideration *today* that any plans we have for integrating this thing called information literacy into the behaviors of information users had better fit in with—mesh the value systems of those users.

So what *is* this thing called information literacy?

The National Forum on Information Literacy is currently addressing the need to define this term. Let me tell you what we are considering at this point. We see information literacy as a chain of related abilities. There are five of them.

First   is the ability to recognize that information is a useful commodity and can help make things better.

Second is the ability to know where to go to get information and whom to ask.

Third   is the ability to retrieve information and to interact with people who have and dispense information.

Fourth   is the ability to interpret, organize, and synthesize information.

Fifth   is the ability to use and communicate, to transfer information.

I think information literacy is a concept worth getting excited about. It is a more holistic concept, than bibliographic instruction, for example, and it suggests an expanded set of responsibilities for information professionals.

Why should a more holistic concept about information be attractive to us? Partly because of the role information is now playing in our lives and partly because of the opportunity this *presents* to the information professional.

With respect to the role of information, we have a litany of facts, some of which, unfortunately, have become limp, meaningless clichés, we hear and repeat them so often:

- our gross national product is now over 50 percent information related.
- Ninety percent of all the scientists who ever lived are alive now, and publishing.
- By mid-decade 60 percent of the work force will earn their living creating, processing or transferring information.
- We are choked with overchoice.
- The gap between all that information and our knowledge of it causes information anxiety.
- We need to manage our choices by acquiring relevant information for decision making.
- Democratic forms of government depend upon input from an informed electorate.

It would be no trick to locate cadres of folks who would agree that all this is so, and that now is not a time to be information illiterate.

True. But there are also legions of people who do not connect these truisms with libraries and librarians. Their information seeking behavior does not include recourse to institutional repositories. Even when it does, librarians may never be consulted. Libraries and librarians do not fit in; they are often not central to the value systems of information seekers.

What might be called "Captive Audience Syndrome" can lead some of us to believe that we already *do* what the information literacy advocates seem to be describing as something new. Captive Audience Syndrome is a collection of symptoms exhibited by students of all ages and who are influenced by teachers in the environment to use libraries and media centers. The symptoms are: forced library attendance, zombie-like reactions to traditional library lessons, retrieval rituals that resemble feeding frenzies, and source "body counts." Why you would think grades depended upon such things. Imagine!

When we study this phenomenon, we observe that as soon as teacher requirements end, students revert to whatever their previous library use patterns were. And we learn that something happens to those multitudes of little ones who have sat transfixed during story hours and have scored at the rocket scientist level on library skills tests. One of those things is puberty. Another is that they pass in prodigious numbers and with dogged determination from the ranks of captive audience to the non-user corps which make up 75 percent of our communities. Not everybody is alarmed by these numbers, by the way. They argue that their mission is to serve the 25 percent well. They point out that 100 percent of the community doesn't use the jails, either.

Also, and somewhat parenthetically, not everyone believes that this information literacy is a good thing for everyone. Newspaper articles claim we would starve to death, if it were not for the availability of poorly educated, information illiterate migrant farm workers to harvest the crops. Seems the rest of us have higher aspirations, or no aspirations, job-wise.

When I have told people about my recent sabbatical during which I traveled to several universities and studied efforts to keep at-risk students eligible, some of them remarked that we may be retaining too many students and developing their expectations beyond the marketplace's capacity to absorb them. As a consequence, nobody wants to flip burgers anymore, and there are only so many openings in the yuppie occupations.

I tell you this to emphasize the point that there are those among us who believe that too much education is a bad thing.

Having said that, I hasten to add that information literate persons would probably make better choices about careers than information illiterate ones, so I happen to be in the camp of the information literacy advocates.

Librarians and Information Literacy

What is the role librarians can play in the information literacy movement? Part of the answer to this question will be based upon how we see our mission with respect to the information literacy chain. Again, the ability to know that it would help to have information, to see that information would be useful, is step one. Another part comes from how "they" — our communities — view our role. It is *their* behavior, remember, that in the final analysis determines whether our plans work or not.

This requires consciousness raising, ours and theirs.* It calls for public relations, marketing and follow-up activities.

Step 2 involves knowing where to go and whom to ask, another area where libraries are frequently not identified by even heavy users of information. We have some control over this. We do know how to advertise and we do know how to negotiate questions. Continuing alliances with educators and prompt, useful responses to requests will help us address step 2.

Step 3, the user's ability to *get* information and to interact with librarians and others (parents, bosses, physicians) who have it to give, is achieved when people have successful encounters in information places and with other holders of information. I think we librarians should remove "spoonfeeding" from our glossary of forbidden practices. We should become convinced, I believe, that the important thing is what people *do* with retrieved information. Delivering information is what *we* do best. Handing someone information is not a perversion of our sacred duty; it *is* our sacred duty. And it is the one for which we are best prepared by our training and inclination. If we could earn the reputation for being providers of information, as well as providers of citations, we would find our stock rising.

This is not to deny that in some environments our obligation is to

*For Curran's consciousness raiser, see Figure 1, p. 45.

Information Literacy:
Users, Their Behavior, and the Price of Eggs
Charles Curran
College of Library and Information Science
University of South Carolina

Information behaves

People behave
Values drive behavior
Information literacy = abilities to:
1. realize
2. know where
3. get
4. interpret
5. use

Is it okay not to know?

My current frame of mind and responsibilities prompt me to locate myself where on this continuum?

1	2	3	4	5	6	7	8	9	10
hide	point	teach	teach and show	show	give them cita- tions	give them info	inter- pret on de- mand	give them inter- preted info	write their report

(This is not a continuum! I will not play. Anyhow, it all depends.)

If tomorrow I got the go ahead to plan an *office for interpretation and organization of information* in my library/information agency:
Who would staff it?
Who would be the clients?
What would be the duties of the staff?
What limitations would I set?
Would I charge a fee?

Figure 1.

help people to become self-reliant learners. We do have an educative function, especially in the schools. But the training that is transferable from one library to another is *not* where the 973s are or how to use the catalog.

The most important and the most transferable experiences are pleasant, productive encounters with user friendly librarians. This is not a popular view, especially in bibliographic instruction circles. I expect that there are many of you who would challenge it.

Step 4 in the chain of information literacy abilities is the ability to interpret, organize and synthesize information. Insofar as their clients are concerned, librarians, with the possible exception of special and entrepreneurial ones, often do not get involved at this level. This is the realm of the teacher—somebody else's turf. I say it is ours too, if we want to be involved in information literacy. Intrude on the consciousness of others through involvement. We have catalog, reference, circulation and interlibrary loan departments. Why not an *interpretation and organization* department? This calls for a new role for librarians, perhaps? Exactly. That's the point.

Ability 5 is using and communicating information, which is sometimes considered to be well outside the traditional turf areas for librarians. But two opportunities come to mind. The first is the opportunity to work in the educational arena with teachers who make assignments that require responses from students. Of course, many librarians are already involved in the information retrieval, documentation, and evaluation processes, which accompany these responses—the products produced by students. If we continue to work effectively with teachers at all levels, we can carve out more influential roles for ourselves.

The second is the fact that industry is undertaking more and more of the responsibility for training workers in their respective environments, and this means that the job of education is now undergoing a very consequential shift away from the colleges and universities and toward businesses. They hire or rent their own educators. There's a role here for enterprising librarians who can deliver. Does this mean new alliances must be forged? Will it mean that new answers to the question: "What business are we in?" will have to be forthcoming? Yes to both.

The National Forum is turning its attention now to target groups: education, business, adult learners, etc. One good thing the Forum has decided is to meet these consumer groups on their terms, not ours. It is *their* definitions of reality we have to contend with. Lots of people simply do not buy our definitions. Zweizig and others have been reminding us of this for some years now. In our libraries we information professionals have no trouble winning approving nods from each other when we define information need in *our* terms. But the consumers are out *there,* and we can not define our way in to their consciousness, we have to *behave* our way in and that requires understanding and accounting for their behavior.

This does not mean we have no obligation to try to raise expectations, broaden horizons and ennoble spirits. We may be constrained by this reality but we are not paralyzed by it. The fact is that values can and do change — and so do behaviors. What it *does* mean is that if we want to read for a part in the information society play, we are going to have to learn everybody's lines and movements, not just our own, and also where the props are. What the other players say and do matters. We can not afford to look clumsy or miss our cues.

Information literacy is a survival skill. It helps us all be participants in the most exciting times so far and we know for sure that the times are going to get *excitinger* and *excitinger*.

Toward an Information
Literate Society:
The Challenge for Librarians

The Honorable Major R. Owens

I listened to the last speaker, Dr. Curran, and thought I would just throw away my notes, because they had all those clichés and truisms that you've been hearing for so long. I often say that I sound like a broken record: I always say the same things over and over again; but following Dr. Curran, I think that I should seek some new ground.

You already know that information for decision making is a primary preoccupation of mine. Politicians are people who are very much like librarians in terms of their need for an encyclopedic approach to the world. Everything comes our way. This morning as I drove to my office, a lady came up to me and said, "Do you know there are rats on our street?" The city is digging up, putting in new sewers, and it seems that suddenly there is an increase in rodents. I said, "Well, tell your city councilman." She said, "Ah, you're passing the buck again!" So I said, "No, we'll take care of it." Rats on the street, cars abandoned, advice to students going to law school, you name it, the congressman can never say "no." You must take an encyclopedic approach to the whole world.

Let me just start by talking a minute about what's happening in Washington as we need to move more rapidly to an information literate society. We are slowly waking up to the great education challenge now that President Reagan's truism or cliché — that the primary purpose of the federal government is defense — has begun to wear off a bit, or the need for that kind of mobilization is questioned because of changing events in the world. We slowly are beginning to admit that we don't have to keep pouring half of our budget into defense. It's a very slow process. Out of a $300 billion budget they propose to cut $14 billion. But this morning I noticed that two Republican senators close to the president said, "No, that's a little scandalous, we have to cut a little more." Slowly they will have to admit that we can no longer have the defense budget drive our economy; that pouring vast amounts into weapons is ridiculous and that the real challenge that we face, the challenge of the last ten years of this century and the challenge of the twenty-first century, is education. Our national security is all bound up now with the degree to which our population is educated, is information literate. We need to have the most education possible at every level. The "value added theory" should prevail in that everybody should be educated to some degree because it adds value to that individual and that individual's ability to function in the society for themselves or to function in society in terms of creating something productive. So from one end of the spectrum to the other we need as much education as possible.

We're just waking up to the challenge of that in Washington. We have been admitting begrudgingly that over the last ten years we've watched little nations dominate worldwide in the economic sector. The two countries that the United States of America defeated, Germany and Japan, are dominant in the economic sector. We've watched how they've both done it: the great difference in the way they've proceeded has been in education. The population is not only very literate and skilled but also there are decision makers at the top, who are obviously more literate and use information better than our top decision makers in our top corporations.

Mismanagement at our corporations—lack of vision at the top levels of our society—is a major problem in the way our society is managed, and is the reason we have begun to fall behind and have lost so much ground in terms of the competitive industrial and commercial sector. Industry is looking for answers not only to the question of how to educate the minorities in the inner cities, who they can see to be their future skilled workers to run the factories, to provide the services and to do the things that they need to have done; but they are also looking for answers on how to better educate their top executives. They have had top executives who have wrecked corporations recently, and they can pinpoint it. They don't talk about it publicly, but among themselves they are looking for ways to educate top people better.

We are looking for ways to avoid the kind of debacle that we have with the savings and loan associations scandal where information was very much available at every level and there was a refusal to use information. What does that refusal mean for our society? The savings and loan association matter is a major crisis not recognized and not talked about much in Washington, but it keeps forcing itself on us in terms of what it means to our economy and the danger of a complete collapse in our financial sector if we don't check it somewhere soon. We may have committed over $166 billion — the overall commitment when you add in all the expenses and the cash needed to pay the depositors off, the administration, the time we need to sell off the assets. And the assumption is that the money's going to come back, that the assets are going to be sold at a profit and that we will sell bonds in order to get the cash to take care of that and we'll get it back. The trouble is that the Japanese are the only people who buy bonds and their stock market is beginning to crumble a bit. There are a lot of things involved. In the final analysis, the American taxpayer, each one of us, will pay out between a thousand and fifteen hundred dollars to bail out these banks that have been ruined by mismanagement, by crooked management. Now the head of the operation, Mr. Seidman, is saying that 60 percent of the S&Ls are the way they are because of fraud. The information was there for management and regulators to use in order to avoid doing some of the things they did, but they did it because of the various "old boy" networks, because of the various schemes where you just cream off the money, knowing full well it's all guaranteed by the taxpayers. Every deposit up to $100,000 in a savings and loan association has the guarantee of the taxpayer behind it. So no matter what goes wrong they knew the government would bail them out. The bureaucrats who were hired by the federal government to regulate; the committees of Congress; the Executive Branch — everybody failed to use the information that was constantly coming in to them. So training executives, decision makers, and leaders to use information more effectively and to make decisions morally is as important as training people at lower levels for these skilled jobs that are going to be available in the labor force.

The education challenge is there and the president has accepted it. Going a few steps beyond the previous president, he has offered a little more than rhetoric. He has come out with some detailed proposals; he has a set of "Goals for American Education" that were developed by the Governors and were endorsed by him (see Appendix). The president in his State of the Union Address spent a considerable amount of time with education and he said, "By the year 2000 we intend to be number one in math and science." This is reflective of that concern I talked about before, the fact that we know that we are losing our competitive edge because other nations that are doing a better job in the commercial sector have a better educated population. We talk a lot about Japan, but not only Japan. Taiwan has a population of 19 million people. The balance of payments surplus between Taiwan and the United States means that they are selling more to us than we are selling to them to the tune of $19 billion, and this is a little nation of 19 million people. In Korea also, the productivity is higher. When students in our country are compared with sixteen other industrialized nations, including Korea and Taiwan, Hong Kong, Japan, when we have our very best (not average) science and math students take assessments tests, pitted against their best science and math students, out of sixteen countries, we scored third from the bottom, just above the Philippines. Japan, Germany, Korea were on top. Recognizing all this, the president has wrapped the situation in the flag and we are going to go forward.

I think it's a good move, you know. We're going to go forward and we are going to be number one by the year 2000 in math and science. I applaud that kind of rally 'round the flag. Let's make America number one in math and science. I don't think literature will suffer that much because resources that are put in place to do that will release some resources that can be put into other things. We're going to find that by the year 2000 we have neglected languages, neglected the literature which tells us about how people live and think in other countries and enables us to sell our products better. There are a number of things across the board in respect to education that we should address. So, this president, who says he wants to the be the education president, finally will get around to meaning business. This year he doesn't, because he's put $500 million in new initiatives into the budget and he cuts education $500 million in other places. So, if he really meant to move forward as the Education President and meet the education challenge he certainly wouldn't pull a trick like that. It's still rhetoric until we see a move beyond that.

But I think it's going to happen. The goals have been stated. And they have been adopted. The question is, are librarians and educators considering all the possibilities with the great readiness that this demands from us? What will happen if we jettison so much of the defense budget and begin to really seriously address ourselves to the question of education? Where are the problems? Where are the gaps? I'm sure you can name a lot of places where you can spend the money. Are you sure you can do so in some systematic way? I know we have had a long period of an administration in Washington that was hostile to libraries, and kept putting zero in the budget for anything that was related to libraries, so people stopped dreaming. Many of us gave up on the schemes that we would use to improve service. I think in Brooklyn the dream was that there should be as many branch libraries as there are movie theaters, or filling stations — that kind of accessibility. We've given up on the dream and library branches have been closed. It's kind of hard to think about the future because of all the adversities of the present. So we are in a situation where, if we were told there will be billions available tomorrow for education — and libraries are a critical part of that — can we come forward with the plans and the schemes to really improve education in the process of spending money?

The danger is that when the agenda shifts and they are ready to provide the resources for education, the infrastructure people, the physical infrastructure people will move in. The construction people, the bulldozers and the bricks and mortar people, they will move in and they will start building buildings and they'll start selling us machinery that we don't need and equipment that we don't need and a lot of things will happen to absorb money, if the people who really know the most about information and about education are not ready to tell us how can you move forward to match the Japanese or the Koreans in terms of an education system which greatly improves on the quality and the quantity — the number of people being educated and the quality of education people are receiving. Japan has twenty-six preschool magazines. None of them is sponsored by the government. There are twenty-six preschool magazines which are able to make it in the commercial sector! They pay for themselves because people buy them, read them and use them. Parents are reading twenty-six preschool magazines. How many do we have in this country? Either subsidized or not subsidized, how many magazines are there? What is the implication of that? Well, they say Japanese children are nurtured. They start off to school with a kind of motivation and readiness that enables the schools to leap forward in terms of the input and the kinds of things that they do with the young children. You know a lot of people say they overdo it and children commit suicide and the society has too much pressure. We need not go to that extreme, but what is the implication of a society where parents are very much concerned in great detail about their children from the time they are born and are investing in their education? What do librarians need to know in order to tie into the goals that the governors and the president have set forth? One goal I've told you is that we want to be first in math and science by the year 2000. You've heard the president's State of the Union Address where he said that. He also said we want to have 100 percent literacy by the year 2000. My committee (the Subcommittee on Select Education) wrote a report on goals, and we said 90 percent by the year 2000. We think they took a lot of stuff from us, but went 10 percent more and said we want to have 100 percent literacy by the year 2000.

Another goal is that all children by the year 2000 should have readiness when they enter school. This means that they are going to have a lot of preschool programs, or preschool books and services and parents will be trained to nurture their children. That's a part of the goals. Another goal is that all children will see basic learning in the elementary school. We will have more of them in your libraries look for assignments perhaps as a result of that kind of motivation. In order to tie into that we need to take a look at those goals and start dreaming about what impact it has upon us — parent collections in libraries; services for parents; preschool books and books for children; new systems for homework assignments lest we be overwhelmed. Speaking as a former public librarian, maybe we — school librarians, public librarians and academic librarians — should get together and see how we are going to handle the load, and approach the government with ways in which to do things which would be most useful.

I heard one of the earlier speakers when I came in and she was speaking about users and I realized that I'm no longer a user — I feel like I'm a lazy user. I pick up the phone and I call the Congressional Research Service and I bark out some orders and I say, "You don't have to rush. I don't need it this afternoon, tomorrow morning." I ask all sorts of complicated questions, you know. "How many people have been convicted so far for their role in destroying savings and loan associations?" "How do you get a job with the Resolution Trust Corporation?" Resolution Trust Corporation is the organization that Congress set up to take over the banks and sell off their assets and so forth, and it has become a big bureaucracy. Already, 2,600 people have been hired, and they predict 6,000 before it's all over, and they have no merit system, no civil service. There's no procedure for getting the job. So, you must have to know the Democrat or the Republican. They must have carved it up — wherever it's located. The biggest office is in Texas, because most of the failed S&Ls are in Texas. There are only one or two offices in New Jersey and New York. The Congressional Research Service now knows who I am, and they send word back, "You expand our parameters; we haven't even collected that information yet." I don't have to worry about the card catalog or whatever retrieval system you are confronting.

I just wonder, is it unreasonable to say we should try to move toward the day when, getting back to an earlier statement, it's not bad to just hand people information. So we try to move our system to the point where they can get it on the telephone, where you call your order in, go by and pick it up. Why not? Why not dream of a system for the public in general, even for students, where we are placed in the process at a pivotal point, and where the public can depend on us to deliver information, assuming that people are really pursuing activities which require information. If they really are pursuing that education, they deserve that kind of support. And, as the society becomes more complex, as demand for more education is created, people are going to need that kind of support which is more efficient and more effective. When I was in the Brooklyn Library, the most popular service there was the telephone reference service. So, it's not unusual that I should enjoy just getting on the phone and calling the Congressional Research Service. Most people enjoy using telephone reference. But we have boundaries placed on this, certain limitations: we couldn't go beyond the question on the phone. But why do we have to be bound by that? If we had the money, if we had the resources, would you dare to have a pick-up and deliver system where you drive up, as to a McDonald's and other kinds of drive-ins? The information is here; you can pick it up and take it home. Why not?

One hundred percent literacy — isn't that where we started trying to get people to read? The first libraries formed were concerned about reading, whereas we have a very complex society and we ought to become masters of the total spectrum for information. We should be as concerned about films and video tapes and television, the total spectrum of information items. In the end we know better than anyone else that it comes back to the book. In our complex society, many of the tasks that have to be learned could probably be taught without using books, without people being able to read, using video tapes and graphs and charts, but it would probably take you ten times longer to teach those complex tasks when you're not using the book. It would be too inefficient to let education go forward without the basic of the interaction of the mind with the printed page of words. In the end, it all comes back to books. People who make video tapes or films read a lot of books and they set it all up first. You come right back to the fact that any civilized society must depend on the printed page.

The interaction between the printed page and the production of all these other instructional information items, of course, is very important. I think that most important is the fact that, aside from just being literate, everyone is required to go through a lifelong learning process, and libraries, of course are indeed a place for that. There is one goal in the "Goals for American Education" that talks about lifelong learning. In the formal education system, if you enter in kindergarten and go through and get a PhD., it's about twenty-one years that you're in the formal system. If you live to be sixty-five, you see how many years you are not in the formal education system in a classroom setting. So where do you get your education from and where do you rely on resources? The library has the greatest potential there.

We're going to have less and less lip service about information literacy and the need for information literacy, and more and more of the necessity that it be created. There are people who make a lot of money now and who are leaders in our society, and they already understand and use information very well. Our society wouldn't move if we didn't make very good uses of information. The people who are most practical and think they are most hard-nosed in our society use information the most. The most effective and most impressive chain of libraries that we have in this country is one that we seldom talk about, and that is the Defense Technical Information Center. I don't mean the military libraries on the bases that serve the troops, I mean the research library complex that is one of the most effective, impressive systems in the whole world. Probably the Soviet Union has something similar. They know the value of information. They know it very well, and as we move forward to our twenty-first century without the burden of carrying the arms race on our backs, we need to think about that. One of the advantages of the arms race is that it has shown societies how much money they can raise, how much money the government can handle, and if you can do that for the arms race, then why not do it for more productive purposes, education being one of those number one purposes.

As wc go forward and as our society becomes more complex, it won't be just in the area of science; it will be in all other areas—in languages and literature. The president of Czechoslovakia is a writer. The scientists couldn't save that nation. The head of the Soviet Union now is a lawyer. Brezhnev was a scientist, an engineer, and he took them under. So science and math still have their place, but this exaltation of science and math is going to get its comeuppance soon. In our society, of course you know, some of the richest people probably didn't get past ninth grade algebra. I don't know what Bill Cosby's education was, but he's a millionaire, and he's not a scientist and he doesn't manufacture anything. Michael Jackson is probably a billionaire. What does he manufacture? Rock artists who are penetrating international cultures don't know anything about math and science. What is the commodity that they're selling? Where do we come in, in terms of producing creativity? Can you keep any rhyming dictionaries in public libraries where there are rap artists around? I'm sure they have taken all the rhyming dictionaries out, and they're buying rhyming dictionaries in great quantities. They're running out of rhymes because everybody is reading the same rhyming dictionary! Their music is going to have to take some new turn. Creativity — that's just another direction. Think of filmmakers. All kinds of things are happening, and there's a world demand for those products, as well as the demand for cars and refrigerators. You know, a refrigerator's a refrigerator's a refrigerator. They are manufactured the same way, whether in Taiwan or Japan or New York. But these cultural products are going to require a great deal of understanding of the new kind of interaction, and the new unexplored landscape of the human mind and the human psyche, and how you appeal to peoples.

I'm going to conclude and say that as we move forward to realize all of these education goals, in the new age blooming, as Washington admits that defense is all won and education is in, I hope that we will strive to be on the front lines of decision making, that we will be aggressive, assert ourselves and insist that when decisions are being made about how to improve education, that the construction industry doesn't come and take 90 percent of the money, and that the decision making is made about real education and about what is needed. The purchase of books and the development of new systems for media impact on youngsters, developing new ways for bibliographic instruction and interaction, and just improving and streamlining services — all will cost money, and somebody has to sit there and demand that that money be appropriated.

At last, the Library Service Construction Act has been approved, and is now ready for the signature of the president. Unfortunately, the chairman of the committee (I'm not chairman of the committee — I'm just sitting on the Post-Secondary Education Committee) decided that we really don't need to do very much with this act because there is going to be a White House Conference on Libraries, and the delegates are going to make all the decisions about where libraries are going, so we can wait five years and come back and do this bill later. I thought this was a great rationalization for a cop-out, because he didn't want to do anything. And having gone through the procedure of the last White House Conference on Libraries and seen all the glorious things which were proposed and how few were done, or even attempted — the batting average was probably as light as ten — I think we are further behind. I challenged the chairman. I said, "We can't wait that long." We had a few sparring matches and finally the chairman beat me down, but I was able to get one thing in called family learning centers.

Let's go forward with the concept that I call family learning centers, where we provide a grant to bring together these services for parents and pay for the library to have a computer that people can come in and practice on, so that the father who might be on a job that needs computer literacy can have that available. A diversity of activities is already there. Some libraries have education information centers, career information centers, parent centers — they already have those kinds of activities. This grant program is meant to bring them all together in one package and to spur experiments in encouraging parents to come into libraries, where transportation is easy, with open hours on weekends and holidays.

The program went through the Reagan process, and got through with a measly $6 million which has to be split with the literacy centers, so it's only $3 million. But it is an example of where we ought to start looking in terms of public libraries. We ought to be on the cutting edge and say to people that in the new society that demands so much of you, a large part of your readiness problems can be solved at the library. We ought to be able to have some models that we can point to when we go through the budget process in the municipalities or on the college campuses, so that you can point to those models and be able to say that you want to be at the decision-making table. We want to demand a share of the resources that are being made available, and we want to know how to direct them. Our dreams and our fantasies that we put on paper, they are here and we can go forward and be the kind of leaders in this information society, this age of information, that only we as librarians can be. I want to close by finishing up with the story Pat Schuman referred to when she introduced me, that is, my fantasy of the martian ship landing and the aliens saying, "Take us to your librarian." It was all about the fact that they came from an advanced civilization, obviously more advanced than ours, because they could land a ship from Mars here. Their civilization, that has surpassed anything we have here on earth, had got that way because of their great appreciation of information. In their society, the librarians were in charge. That is our goal.

Discussion

Panel and Audience

James D. Anderson, Associate Dean, Rutgers SCILS: I have a comment on Dr. Dalrymple's paper. You set up a contrast between bibliographic instruction and systems design. I think the real problem is the way we manage our resources and what we choose to do with them. I was intrigued with your reference to the supercatalog, and it reminded me of descriptions of catalogs by Charles Ami Cutter, about a hundred years ago. Those catalogs had lots of analytics for parts of books and parts of journals, and that basically describes the supercatalog. The catalog he talked about also provided a kind of lead-in vocabulary so that people would have alternative ways to search for topics or subjects. We sometimes refer to our current generation of catalogs as "moving." Our catalogs are less than that, they are "limping," because most of them have thrown out the lead-in vocabulary. If there is anything that we know, it is the enormous human variety of ways of expressing ideas and subjects and topics, and of course you were addressing this.

My favorite bottom line is some Bell Labs research that summarized the whole thing: that you need about fifteen different ways to express a topic to get 80 percent of the queries to match. Yet we've thrown that out. So there are lots of things we know that we don't choose to implement.

The last example I want to cite concerns this Boolean business. Boolean logic belongs in mathematics and it doesn't work for searching. A weighted kind of searching where you make a prediction on the best answers to questions based on characteristics of the sources, and you give a ranked response, is something we have known about for several decades, but very, very few systems touch upon it.

Dalrymple: Everything that goes around, comes around. I've really been quite struck by what you say. We've known many of these things for an awfully long time, and what is a really intriguing question — and I certainly don't have the answer to it — is, why have we not acted on the knowledge? Possibly it is a question of resources. The technology is there.

Quinn: There have been software programs out there which had the ranking algorithms in them. They were not used, so the systems people took them away. The users did not take advantage of them, but I don't know why.

Dalrymple: I tested a system when I worked in a medical library that gave the user a probabilistic retrieval algorithm, and the users really liked what was called "soft Boolean." But the people who did not like it were the librarians and the scientists who had had some exposure to traditional information retrieval. This is an area I would like to investigate further — it is mysterious why people have the reactions that they do.

Diane Reed Klaiber, AT&T: I think that everybody is saying the same thing, but Dr. Curran put it in a nutshell when he said that the bottom line is to tune in to the values of our customers. Just recently this hit home with us. In AT&T, we have felt that we are on the leading edge of the electronic library and that we know what our users should be doing with electronic libraries. Recently we held some focus interviews with our customers, and found that they do not necessarily want electronic services — they don't want another system that they have to use. They want to go to their librarian, and have that person get the information for them. So I am in a quandry, running an information center where we are downsizing, where we charge for our services, and yet our customers are saying that they want value-added service, and don't want to learn another system. We may be in the electronic information age, but we have different users out there, and we need to hone in on their values, as Dr. Curran says. The question is, how do I as a manager handle that, given the restraints of the economy?

Owens: I think that you need more money to hire more staff so that you can have technicians who do that for people. I wasn't kidding when I said the Congressional Research Service approach should not be a luxury. We should move in the direction of handing people what they need. The electronic systems are efficient for librarians, because they know how to use them. There are tasks simpler than electronic retrieval that technicians can perform. Why can't we move toward a state where we have the personnel to provide the services? That costs money, and

I think we are used to an economy of scarcity, and don't even think of those possibilities.

Danilo Figueredo, Executive Director, New Jersey Library Association: Listening to speakers who represent such widely different worlds, who deal with high-tech information systems on the one hand and with basic literacy needs on the other, has called up conflicting images for me. One of Karen Takle Quinn's information system diagrams reminded me of Jorge Luis Borges' classic short story about the library of Babylon, and I have also thought about Alan Bloom's *The Closing of the American Mind* and Richard Rodriguez's *Hunger of Memory.* The strongest image, however, takes me back to about a decade ago, when I was at the Newark Public Library, working on a project to get books in the hands of Spanish speaking kids and adults. There was one person who said that getting a book into the hands of kids whose parents don't know how to read and who have a family income of $5,000 or $6,000, was not going to do anything for those kids. The reason that this came to mind was that I recently saw one of those kids I knew ten years ago roaming the streets of New Brunswick, and he seems to be either homeless or without a place to go. We need the high-tech world, but we have to hang on to the human aspect of what we are trying to do. Even though we don't always succeed in reaching people, one single librarian might have an impact on an individual, who someday might become something like a writer, another Piri Thomas of *Down These Mean Streets,* who can then inspire others. I don't want to get so much into this technology that we forget that.

Curran: Lots of times we librarians are naïve, and we forge ahead because we are convinced of the wonderfulness of our systems. This is a personal war story, from a time when I was at a school where the major curricula were health and physical education. Most of the students were majoring in towels. They came in for bibliographic instruction because it was that time of year. So I would point to Charles Evans' *American Bibliography, Checklist of American Imprints* — everything you could ever want to know that was ever published in what is now the United States of America from 1639 to 1820, right there in those maroon boxes. And they would just mouth-breathe. I was not plugging onto their value system. If I could have taught them about the comparative method for leading off first base, I would have been plugging into their value system. I think that we get naïve about the wonderfulness that we find ourselves working with; we forget sometimes that others are not so impressed.

Elyse Robinson, Merck: I understand what Major Owens was saying about providing information. I am a patent information specialist. I give the information directly to the attorneys I work with. I know exactly what you are talking about — handing information to people — but I came from somewhere, somebody had to train me. The question I have is, how are we going to train people to provide information in this way, so that the client can rely on it?

Luis Rodriguez, Montclair State College: In regard to giving information directly to the end user, one thing I see information literacy doing is enabling the end user to evaluate that information. That is one role our bibliographic instruction courses should play. Not necessarily how to find the information, but once you find it, how to evaluate it. So that when lawyers get patent information, they have a good sense of whether it was a complete search or not.

Kuhlthau: There is an even more basic issue here, and that is having a person actually understand the need for information. Three fourths of the population really doesn't have a sense of when they need information, nor that there is information available for them to go get. This problem seems to me to be a large part of what we used to call bibliographic instruction. Being information literate is actually knowing when you need information and that there is a world of information that can help you.

Schuman: We've been talking a lot about how to understand the user and how to understand the technology. I think you also have to understand how information is created. There is a great danger that we face in embracing electronic information. There is a lot of information that is not available electronically. Five companies control 90 percent of sales and use of data bases. This is one of the things I think the library field has not addressed enough. So while we talk about this great universal access, I think we have to consider what it is that we are going to get access to.

Joy Moll, Stockton State College: I have a comment based on both experience and research. When I did my doctoral dissertation, I was interested in how subject access to children's materials was provided. I discovered to my horror that standard Library of Congress children's headings were at a reading level much higher than that of the material they were meant to give access to. As a result of this research, I had to conclude that we were trying to teach children to use a tool they could not read. But I have come to another conclusion in the years since, which relates to what Carol Kuhlthau was saying about bibliographic instruction and what Karen Takle Quinn said about using electronic systems. We are using computer conferencing now to team teach in our schools, and with our commuting students at Stockton, we find electronic mail very useful. I have found that there are people who need to get sources of information quickly and easily, so that they can get on with evaluating the information. And then there are the really heavy users, whom we must train so that they themselves can use the systems so that we can all save time. There are different levels of needs and use, and training must take these differences into account.

Hilary Crew, Rutgers SCILS student: My question is closely aligned with the last one. Children are being asked to use electronic information systems designed for adults. I wonder how much research has been done, for instance, on the use of online catalogs by children? Obviously they are going to have more difficulty with terminology and formulating searches.

Quinn: I know of some work that is being done in a San Joaquin, California, elementary school where they have an online catalog.

Nancy Kuntz Cornell, Middlesex Public Library: I came to this symposium for a particular reason. Although I have always considered myself to be an information literate person, I am in a situation where I need more ammunition with which to combat a young man who is running for public office in my town. He was quoted in the newspaper as saying that we don't need a librarian for our elementary school, just more books. In my own work as a librarian, sometimes I point people to sources, and sometimes I give the information to the student who seems incapable of using anything, in the hopes that next time when he comes back, I will have more time to give him a little instruction on how to use the card catalog. During this symposium, I have found several arguments that I can take back and use to persuade this politician that we really do need a librarian for our elementary school.

Information Literacy:
A Subject Source Survey and
Annotated Bibliography

Howard M. Dess

Introduction

What is information literacy and why are librarians and educators so concerned about it? Two recent events are illustrative: (1) President-elect Barbara Ford of ACRL chose information literacy as the theme of her 1990–1991 tenure in office. (2) The ALA established a Presidential Committee on Information Literacy whose final report issued in 1989 provided fundamental definitions (". . . information-literate people are those who have learned how to learn. . . . They are people prepared for lifelong learning. . . ."), proposed a new model for education based on the information sources of the "real world," and offered recommendations for actions that would spur the introduction and implementation of information literacy programs in the U.S.

The fact that these influential and prestigious organizations are supporting the cause of information literacy is a measure of the importance that this concept has assumed in the 1980s and indicative of the intellectual ferment currently associated with it. The genesis of this vigorous campaign to promote information literacy may be traced to the appearance of a notable publication, one that shook librarians out of whatever complacency they may have hitherto enjoyed about the presumably secure role of libraries in our society. That publication was *A Nation at Risk: The Imperative for Education Reform* by the National Commission on Excellence in Education (1983). Librarians were dismayed to discover that this report failed to include a role for libraries in its overview of the educational reforms recommended for advancing the development of the "learning society." This alarming and inexplicable omission served to galvanize a number of individuals in the library community who began writing extensively about their vision of libraries as vital resources for the lifelong educational process, resources that must be fully incorporated into any plan for educational reform.

Guide to the Bibliography

For an informative overview of recent work on information literacy, the review article entitled "Information Literacy: An Introductory Reading List" by Trish Ridgeway is an excellent starting point. A prior review article by Carol Kuhlthau *(Information Skills for an Information Society: A Review of Research)* provides even more extensive documentation about relevant research work and the historical development of this concept.

A recent book coauthored by Patricia Senn Breivik and Gordon Gee, *Information Literacy: Revolution in the Library,* offers a comprehensive discussion of information literacy in all its ramifications and presents compelling arguments for the need to integrate libraries into the educational process. This book should be considered as essential reading for anyone interested in the subject of information literacy. This same theme is the subject of Issue No. 24 of *The Reference Librarian,* edited by Maureen Pastine and Bill Katz. Entitled *Integrating Library Use Skills into the General Education Curriculum,* it contains a collection of twenty-six articles by librarians, educators, and administrators who discuss a variety of ways and means to promote the development and implementation of information literacy programs.

An earlier very influential book, by Ernest L. Boyer, entitled *College: The Undergraduate Experience in America,* is included in the bibliography because it is so frequently cited on its findings about the manner in which most college and university curricula appear to ignore (or at best underutilize) the rich abundance of information resources available in their campus libraries, and the concomitant negative implications of these observations as regards the development of information literacy skills among our students.

Various authors and researchers have grappled with definitions of information literacy. The American Library Association's *Final Report* on information literacy provides an authoritative and "official" definition which appears to embody a consensus viewpoint that most librarians and educators can agree with. Not surprisingly, however, various shades of opinion can be found in the literature of this subject. Thus, Lori Arp has questioned whether information literacy is simply a new name for bibliographic instruction. However, Hannelore Rader argues that bibliographic instruction should be considered as an evolutionary way station along the path to the development of information literacy. Variation in nomenclature across national boundaries was noted by Kirk and Alp who discussed the preference for the phrase "information skills" in Australia and the UK as opposed to information literacy. However, they recommended a switch to the use of the latter.

Still other authors have compared and contrasted computer literacy with information literacy, and in this case several distinct points of view have emerged. One school of thought represented by authors such as Forest Woody Horton, Jr., D. L. Layman, E. Mortensen, and E. M. Trauth (1983) consider information literacy to be a much broader concept, which incorporates computer literacy as a subset. As stated in other terms by Layman in 1983, computer literacy places more emphasis on the tool rather than the information retrieved by the tool. However, authors such as Hartsuijker or Jerome Johnstone or Plomp and Carleer appear to consider these two categories as related but independent entities of nearly equal importance in the educational process.

Numerous descriptions of information literacy programs have been published. Examples of such programs in the U.S. can be found in works by Mary Beth Allen, Patricia Senn Breivik, Karen Hoelscher, Barbara MacAdam, Suzanne Maranda, Charles Martell, and Hannelore Rader. However, the U.S. is not the only country where information literacy programs have been introduced into the educational system. The Netherlands has been particularly active in formulating and implementing such programs, as discussed in articles by Hartsuijker, by Plomp and Carleer, by E. M. Trauth (1986), and by Van Weering and coworkers. Programs in Australia and the UK are summarized by Joyce Kirk. Work in Canada is presented in an article by Suzanne Maranda, and Mioduser, et al. describe what has been done in Israel. Finally, articles about the need for information literacy programs in underdeveloped countries such as India or various African states are discussed by R. M. Mathew, and by Adakole Ochai.

Methodology Used to Survey the
Literature on Information Literacy

Most of the citations listed in this bibliography were obtained via a very extensive online search of the DIALOG family of databases. Some recent online innovations introduced by DIALOG in 1990 greatly facilitated this task. First, it is now possible to search *all* the files listed in DIALINDEX (file 411) via one simple command: SF ALL. This type of search was carried out for the phrase "information() (literate or literacy)" and a total of 258 hits was retrieved, contained in 45 files (out of a total of 291 files searched). Secondly, the total number of hits retrieved can now be ranked, by file, in descending order of hits retrieved, via the command: RANK FILES. The results obtained are listed (in part) below, for the top 10 files only, which contained 179 hits or 69.4 percent of the total:

Hits	File #	Description
43	1	ERIC, 1966–90
23	647	Magazine ASAP, 1983–90
22	202	Information Sci. Abs., 1966–90
17	61	LISA, 1969–90
17	648	Trade and Indust. ASAP, 1983–90
15	6	NTIS, 1964–90
12	13	INSPEC, 1977–90
11	239	MathSci, 1959–90
10	440	Current Contents Search, 1989–90
9	8	Compendex Plus, 1970–90

This ranked listing is helpful in showing which online files are most relevant to the subject under investigation. In the present case, ERIC is clearly the single most important file. Next, the top twenty files on this ranked list (containing 88.4 percent of the total hits) were searched simultaneously via DIALOG's One-Search feature. The final step in the online search process was to eliminate duplicate retrievals by applying the RD command (remove duplicates) to the answer set, which reduced the number of hits to 153. These were then printed out in full and individually examined for content and relevance. In this manner an additional 85 answers were discarded for reasons such as the following:

* The largest category of discards were those hits that focused primarily or exclusively on computer literacy. By way of comparison, the literature on computer literacy is vastly larger than that on information literacy. An ALL FILES search in DIALINDEX on the phrase

"computer() (literate or literacy)" yielded 15,157 hits, a result that was nearly sixty-fold larger than that obtained for information literacy.

* A smaller number of the discards were simply false drops, non-relevant answers retrieved because of quirks in indexing or syntax.
* A very few of the discards were additional duplicate answers that had not been winnowed out earlier by DIALOG's detection algorithm.

In this fashion, the 258 answers originally retrieved online were pruned down to a collection of 68 papers and documents, to which were added some recent articles that had not yet been picked up by any online indexing or abstracting service. This core group then served as the "mother lode" that was mined selectively to produce the annotated bibliography presented in the next section.

As a caveat to the reader, this bibliography should not be viewed as comprising an exhaustive record about information literacy. Rather, the principal objective was to provide an informative overview of the literature on the subject that would serve as an introduction for the reader interested in learning more about the field, how it developed and evolved over the years, who are some of the major contributors, what are they advocating, and what progress has been made to date in implementing relevant programs.

Bibliography

Allen, Mary Beth. *Information Literacy, the Library and the Basic Reader/Writer.* Paper, 38th annual meeting of the Conference on College Composition and Communication, Atlanta, March 19–21, 1987. ED 284580.

Describes and discusses a bibliographic instruction program offered by the University of Illinois Undergraduate Library for students enrolled in freshman English courses. The program incorporates several basic concepts: (1) Information is formally structured according to subject hierarchies, (2) the student body is heterogeneous so that different groups have different needs, and (3) the program is integrated into the curriculum. Students are introduced to the idea of doing their own research, via a controlled exercise designed by librarians and writing instructors.

Altan, Susan. *Desperately Seeking Standards. Creating Competent College-Bound Library Users.* Based on papers presented at the

16th National LOEX Library Instruction Conference, Bowling Green, May 1988, and the Ohio Educational Library Media Association Conference, Columbus, October 1988. ED 307894.

The development of information literacy skills in college bound students would be aided by the development and application of standards covering this aspect of their education. Such standards could serve as a basis for high school programs aimed at improving students' proficiency in research skills, and might also be incorporated into college admission criteria.

American Library Association Presidential Committee on Information Literacy. *Final Report.* Chicago: ALA, January 1989.

ALA's official policy document on information literacy. It offers a definition of information literacy, discusses its importance to individuals in all aspects of their personal and professional lives and to the well-being of the nation as a whole. Recommendations for actions to promote information literary focus on educational reforms that actively engage the students in the exposure to and utilization of the broadest range of information resources such as online databases, videotapes, government documents, journals, etc.

Arp, Lori. "Information Literacy or Bibliographic Instruction: Semantics or Philosophy?" *RQ* 30 (Fall 1990): 46–49.

A cogent questioning and comparison of the definitions, objectives, and anticipated outcomes associated with information literacy programs vs. bibliographic instruction. Are they the same? "In some ways" is the conclusion reached by the author, who probes deeply into the fundamental concepts underlying each of these spheres of activity. However, ambiguities associated with both are still a source of confusion and should be clarified via further research.

Barron, Daniel D. "Resources-Based Education, Technology, Information Literacy, and Libraries: Views from Other Associations and the Government." *School Library Media Activities Monthly* 6 (October 1989): 46–50.

A review of nineteen recent publications from professional associations and the federal government about school library media programs and media specialists as related to information literacy.

Benenfeld, Alan R. "Information Literacy: Awareness of and Access to Information Resources." Paper included in public service booklet by American Society for Information Science entitled *Eight Key Issues for the White House Conference on Library and Information Services.* Washington, DC: ASIS, 1978.

This paper offers an early discussion of the concept of information literacy.

Black, Shirley Ulferts. "Educational Reform and Libraries: A Report and Bibliography." *RQ* 29 (Spring 1989): 321–24. (Presented as a contribution to the *Library Literacy* section, edited by Mary Reichel.)

The author reports on a Southeastern Michigan conference which focused on developments in academic libraries since the publication of *A Nation at Risk* in 1983. Summaries of the key papers all emphasized the importance of integrating school libraries firmly into the educational process and the need for librarians to function as educators as well as information providers. The annotated bibliography contains works selected on the basis of their impact on the discussion between librarians and other educators about the future of libraries in the educational reform debate.

Boyer, Ernest L. *College: The Undergraduate Experience in America.* New York: Harper, 1987.

Sponsored by the Carnegie Foundation for the Advancement of Teaching, this highly cited work has served as an influential resource document and motivational spur for educators and librarians alike. Although the subject of information literacy is not discussed as such, Boyer's findings about the virtual exclusion of the academic library from the college curriculum are profoundly disturbing and have served to provide evidentiary support for new programs and proposals aimed at reversing this underutilization. Boyer himself urges an integration of the school library with the classroom so that the library may function as an essential learning resource in the educational process.

Breivik, Patricia Senn. "Making the Most of Libraries in the Search for Academic Excellence." *Change* 19 (July/August 1987): 44–52.

An article directed specifically at educators and educational administrative leaders. It summarizes the proceedings of the Arden

House Symposium (see Breivik and Wedgeworth below) which focused on the benefits to be derived from better and more creative use of libraries in the educational system. Examples are presented of successful programs where libraries have worked in partnership with academic departments to develop beneficial new ways to enrich the learning experience of students.

_____, ed. *A Colorado Response to the Information Society: The Changing Academic Library.* Proceedings, October 6–7, 1983, Denver. ED 269017.

The purpose of this conference was to explore the role of academic libraries in the information society. Seven papers were presented by librarians, educators, and academic administrators from a diverse group of U.S. institutions of learning. All dealt with various aspects of information literacy.

_____, and Gordon E. Gee. *Information Literacy: Revolution in the Library.* New York: American Council on Education/Macmillan, 1989.

This remarkable book, almost evangelical in its fervor, "...is dedicated to the concept that, in today's information society, the active involvement and support of academic libraries will be a key to achieving higher education reform goals." The authors build a powerful case for integrating academic libraries into the curriculum as the best way to promote information literacy within the educational process. In order to achieve this goal, they emphasize the necessity to gain the full support and backing of educational leaders and administrators at the highest institutional levels. The style of presentation is exceptionally clear and easy to read. The book is heavily documented and serves a valuable secondary purpose as a comprehensive reference source to related work on this subject.

_____, and Robert Wedgeworth, eds. *Libraries and the Search for Academic Excellence.* Metuchen, NJ: Scarecrow, 1988.

Papers from the national Symposium on Libraries and the Search for Academic Excellence, March 15–17, 1987, at Columbia University's Arden House, co-sponsored with the University of Colorado. The purpose was to address recent educational reform reports, and to review the role of libraries in achieving academic goals. Included are papers by U.S. Rep. Major Owens, Ernest

Boyer, Frank Newman, other educators and librarians. One of the action agenda items which conclude these proceedings led to the ALA's presidential commission on information literacy.

Demo, William. "The Idea of Information Literacy in the Age of High-Tech." Unpublished paper, Tompkins Cortland Community College, Dresden, New York, 1986. ED 282537.

Information literacy is defined as a new intellectual skill that will enable us to be masters of new communications and information technologies. However, the author is also critical of certain aspects of information technology that may hinder the broadest development of information literacy among the population at large. Factors specifically noted include information over-supply, costs associated with online operations, and invisibility of the information revolution to the average person. Schools, public libraries, and academic libraries must play a major role in promoting information literacy.

Fennell, Janice C., ed. *Building on the First Century.* Proceedings of the 5th National Conference of the Association of College and Research Libraries, Cincinnati, April 5–8, 1989. Chicago: ACRL, 1989.

Information literacy and bibliographic instruction comprise one of nine subject categories covered during this conference. Individual papers in this group address topics such as working with faculty, course-integrated library instruction, program evaluation, teaching methods, and learning styles.

FitzSimmons, J. J. "The Information Millennium." *Information Society* 5 (January 1987): 51–55.

Humankind's third millennium is viewed as an era in which information will be the key strategic resource. The author believes that information literacy will be one of the most important policy issues involved in shaping the future of society.

Ford, Barbara J. "Information Literacy." *College and Research Library News* 9 (November 1989): 892–93.

Discusses the role of the American Library Association in taking a leadership position for developing and advancing information literacy in the United States. Reviews and summarizes definitions and recommendations for information literacy programs promulgated by ALA, and specifies information literacy as the theme for her presidency of ACRL.

Hamelink, Cees. "An Alternative to News." *Journal of Communication* 26 (Autumn 1976): 120–24.
The author emphasizes the need for alternative information networks to offset the oppressive effects of the institutionalized public media and discusses a program for acquiring information literacy.

Hartsuijker, Ard P. "Development of Computer and Information Literacy in the Netherlands." *Education and Computing* 2 (1986): 89–93.
The author describes a national project on computer and information literacy in the Netherlands for all students in the twelve-to-sixteen-year-old age group. Curriculum development is discussed with emphasis on equal participation by teachers and students.

Hine, Betsy N., et al. "Bibliographic Instruction for the Adult Student in an Academic Library." *Journal of Continuing Higher Education* 37 (Spring 1989): 20–24.
Description and discussion of an adult education program at the University of Evansville which encourages the development of information literacy in its students as a means of promoting lifelong learning.

Hoelscher, Karen. "Computing and Information: Steering Student Learning." *Computers in the Schools* 3 (Spring 1986): 23–34.
Discusses the Minnesota Education Computing Corporation's Computing and Information Collection. This is a collection of software products for students in grades 4–12. These products are designed to enable students to develop and practice information literacy skills in the context of school curricular programs.

Horton, Forest Woody, Jr. "The Knowledge Center." *Information Management* 19 (February 1985): 20, 22.
The author argues that business firms would be well advised to shift the emphasis of their information departments away from computer literacy to information literacy. He advocates the introduction of information literacy training programs for employees that would convert information departments into knowledge centers.

_____. "Information Literacy vs. Computer Literacy." *ASIS Bulletin* 9 (April 1983): 14–16.

A business oriented article that emphasizes the need to expand our horizons beyond computer literacy to encompass information literacy as a means of amplifying a firm's intellectual resources "a hundred-fold." Also provides a useful differentiation between computer literacy and information literacy.

Huston, Mary M. "Extending Information Universes Through Systems Thinking." *College and Research Library News* 51 (September 1990): 692–95.

In this first of a proposed series of articles on information literacy, the author posits the concept that "...a fundamental definition of information literacy must acknowledge the value of knowing how to navigate systems that affect our everyday existence...." She reviews the information seeking process and relates it to several models of information systems representative of varying degrees of complexity and sophistication.

Johnston, Jerome. *Information Literacy: Academic Skills for a New Age.* National Institute of Education, Washington, D.C., 1985. ED 270042.

The now pervasive distribution of computer technology in our society has wrought changes in the educational process that require new skills both for students and teachers. Computer literacy and information literacy are both important in higher education and the workplace after graduation. The author identifies and discusses various issues relating to these topics.

Jongejan, T., S. Cory, and V. Smith. "So Your District Has Mandated Computer Literacy: What Do You Do Now?" Paper in *Computers in Education,* Proceedings of the IFIP TC 3, 4th World Conference, Norfolk, VA, July 29–August 2, 1985. New York: Elsevier, 1985.

Description and discussion of an experiment to define the content of computer and information literacy programs in junior high schools in the Netherlands.

Kanter, J. "Information Literacy for the CEO." *Journal of Information Systems Management* 5 (Winter 1988): 52–57.

A discussion of techniques that information systems managers can use to help enhance or improve information literacy skills in the top executive ranks of their firms.

Kirk, J., and P. Alp, eds. "Information Literacy and Information Technology," Paper in *Australian Computers in Education Conference Proceedings,* September 26–28, 1988, Perth, Australia. Mount Lawley, Western Australia: Educational Computer Association of Western Australia, 1988.

In Australia and the UK, the term "information skills" is more generally used in the literature of education rather than "information literacy." A discussion and analysis of this usage leads the authors to recommend "information literacy" as the preferred terminology since it is more inclusive, and embodies the skills, knowledge and attitudes which are essential for the effective use of information by individuals.

Kirk, Joyce. "Information Skills in Schools." *Australian Library Journal* 36 (May 1987): 82–87.

Discusses the need to teach information skills (as opposed to library) skills in elementary and secondary schools and describes some of the curriculum policies and courses developed by schools in the UK and Australia.

Kuhlthau, Carol C. "The Information Search Process of High-Middle-Low Achieving High School Seniors." *School Library Media Quarterly* 17 (Summer 1989): 224–28.

The author suggests that new educational approaches are required to teach students how to become effective information users. This conclusion grew out of a study carried out on the information search process of a group of high school seniors.

————. *Information Skills for an Information Society: A Review of Research.* Syracuse, NY: ERIC Clearinghouse on Information Resources, 1987. ED 297740.

A comprehensive overview and summary of research literature concerned with the definition, characteristics, and development of information literacy both in the U.S. and internationally. Emphasis is placed on school media centers as a focal point for integrating skills and resources across the curriculum and allowing students to develop a proficiency in inquiry that will enable them to lead productive, meaningful lives.

Kwatra, P. S. "2001: An Information Society." *Herald of Library Science* 22 (January 1983): 62–65.

Defines information-conscious and information-literate societies and discusses how the new technology is expected to alter the characteristics of information systems and what concomitant changes will be required in our educational infrastructure.

Layman, D. L. "Information Literacy and Educational Productivity." Paper in *Proceedings of the 46th ASIS Annual Meeting* October 2–6, 1983, Arlington, VA. White Plains, N.Y.: Knowledge Industry Publications, 1983.

The prevailing enthusiasm for computer literacy in schools places excessive emphasis on an information tool rather than on the information itself. Improvements in problem solving and decision making require information literacy, defined as an understanding of how knowledge is created, distributed, and used.

MacAdam, Barbara. "Information Literacy: Models for the Curriculum." *College and Research Library News* 51 (November 1990): 948–51.

Describes and discusses courses on information gathering and bibliographic instruction recently introduced into the curriculum at the University of Michigan for communications majors and MLS matriculants. Some of the concepts and instructional techniques utilized in these courses are recommended for consideration as possible curriculum models for the development of new academic programs and services specifically designed to promulgate information literacy in future generations of students.

Maranda, Suzanne. "Developing the Role of the End-User Librarian." *Bibliotheca Medica Canadiana* 10 (no. 3, 1989): 126–29.

The author describes an information literacy program introduced at the Bracken Health Sciences Library, Queen's University, Kingston, Ontario. The objective of this program is to equip students with the knowledge and ability to use the full range of tools available for accessing, retrieving, and managing information throughout their careers. The role of librarians as end-user educators is emphasized.

Martell, Charles, et al. "Hard Facts, Hard Work: Academic Libraries and 'A Nation at Risk'—A Symposium." *Journal of Academic Librarianship* 14 (May 1988): 72–81.

Reviews issues cited in *A Nation at Risk* and other studies calling for educational reform, and discusses the role of libraries in general, and academic libraries in particular, in improving education in the U.S. library programs involving information literacy, research skills, and peer counseling are described as implemented at three universities.

Masuda, Yoneji. "The Role of the Library in the Information Society." *Electronic Library* 1 (April 1983): 143–47.
   Considers the impact of the future information society on libraries. Information literacy will be an important factor.

Mathew, R. M. "Marketing of Social Science Information and Documentation: The Challenges of the Third World Countries with Special Reference to India." *International Forum on Information and Documentation* 11 (no. 1, 1986): 19–23.
   The author considers information literacy as a valuable resource for development in third world countries. He recommends that national governments should take suitable measures to establish an information infrastructure involving the organization and improvement of information related functions, education and training in information handling and use, and effective and operation of information systems.

Merriam, Joyce. *Helping College-Bound Students Develop Higher Levels of Information Literacy: A Report on a Study of Selected School Library Media Programs in Massachusetts.* August 1988. ED 302235.
   School library media programs have a growing potential to promote the development of higher levels of information literacy in college-bound students, particularly those who have been introduced to electronic technologies that access and retrieve information quickly. Full documentation is provided, plus an extensive bibliography.

Mioduser, David, et al. *The Information Society and the Educational System. Technical Report No. 16.* Tel Aviv University, February 1985. ED 290455.
   This paper describes in detail the design of a complete curriculum in information literacy intended for all students in elementary and junior high schools.

Mortensen, E. "The PC and Online Databases in the Business Environment." Paper in *Proceedings, National Online Meeting 1985*. Medford, N.J.: Learned Information Inc., 1985.

Business managers must be trained to take full advantage of PCs that are now so pervasive in the commercial environment. However, the author argues that computer literacy in itself is not enough: information literacy is required so that managers will be fully aware of the multitude of information sources available to them.

Ochai, Adakole. "The Emerging Information Society." *International Library Review* 16 (October 1984): 367-72.

The author compares and contrasts the development of information literacy in the U.S. versus the situation in the developing countries which lag far behind because they cannot afford the necessary resources.

Otten, Klaus W. "Information Resources Management: Management Focus on the Value of Information and Information Work." *Journal of Information and Image Management* 17 (August 1984): 9-14.

Information resources must now be considered as a factor of production on a par with capital and labor, which, historically, were the principal focal points of classical economic theories. The management of information necessitates the integration of information tools into the work process. Six important steps are described relating to the introduction of information resource management into the business environment, and these steps include infrastructure changes to motivate managers and coworkers toward information literacy.

_____. "Towards an Information Society: A Healthy Information Industry as the Basis for a Stable National Economy." *Journal of Information and Image Management* 17 (December 1984): 51-56.

The author presents an overview of the components of the growing information industry. This industry is seen as the basis for the creation of new jobs and of alternate jobs for those lost as a result of automation in both manufacturing and information work sectors. Information technology and industry are seen as both driving and stabilizing forces which keep the economies of developed nations functioning during the transition from an industrial society to an information society. Evolving development of new information-based professions, services, and products are forseen. Concomitantly, an increasing portion of our time is expected to be preoccupied with continuing education in order to promote information literacy and forestall professional obsolescence.

Pastine, Maureen, and Bill Katz, eds. *Integrating Library Use Skills into the General Education Curriculum.* New York: The Haworth Press, 1989. (Published simultaneously as *The Reference Librarian,* No. 24.)

A collection of papers which describe and discuss numerous topics relevant to information literacy. Subjects covered include bibliographic instruction issues and programs; teaching library skills at various levels of the educational system, from high school through the university; teaching library use skills outside of the educational system; issues related to computers and online searching; the role of the library in development of critical reasoning skills and evaluation of information sources; building on basic library skills to develop more advanced search techniques and provide a sound basis for life-long learning outside the classroom.

Plomp, Tjeerd, and Gerrit Carleer. "Towards a Strategy for the Introduction of Information and Computer Literacy (ICL) Courses." *Computers and Education* 11 (no. 1, 1987): 53–62.

Reviews findings of a national survey to determine how information and computer literacy (ICL) instruction is being introduced into Dutch secondary schools. Factors influencing the successful implementation of educational innovations are discussed, and strategies for future implementation of ICL courses are presented.

Rader, Hannelore B. "Bringing Information Literacy into the Academic Curriculum." *College and Research Libraries News* 51 (October 1990): 879–80.

Description of an information literacy program that was initiated by the Cleveland State University Library as part of a broader curriculum revision introduced by the university. The information literacy program builds on, and is an expansion of an already existing bibliographic instruction program.

———. "Bibliographic Instruction or Information Literacy?" *College and Research Libraries News* 51 (January 1990): 18–20.

The author contends that information literacy is a much broader concept than bibliographic instruction. Information literacy is intended to "...prepare people for lifelong self-education in a global electronic environment, ... to handle information effectively in any given situation even outside of a library environment; ... to organize information critically and productively..." regardless of the source. From a historical perspective, she argues that "...bibliographic instruction is part of an evolution toward information literacy, just as library orientation and library instruction was a step toward the evolution of BI."

Ridgeway, Trish. "Information Literacy: An Introductory Reading List." *College and Research Library News* 51 (July/August 1990): 645–48.

An excellent starting point for anyone seeking an introduction to the subject of information literacy. The reading list is divided into five major subject categories: (1) Definition of information literacy, (2) publications aimed at nonlibrarians, (3) publications for librarians, (4) information literacy in the schools, and (5) program descriptions. Contains twenty-seven references.

Schiffman, Shirl S. "Influencing Public Education: A 'Window of Opportunity' Through School Library Media Centers." *Journal of Instructional Development* 10 (no. 4, 1988): 41–44.

Suggests that instructional technology theory and practice can be introduced into the public schools through the school library media center. The media specialist is discussed as an agent for change and related to the development of information literacy in the schools.

Sorg, James D., and Edward P. Laverty. "Information Technology and Education for the Public Service." *International Journal of Public Administration* 8 (December 1986): 391–408.

The authors express concern that most graduate programs in public administration/affairs do not educate their students in information technology. Curricular revision is recommended that would incorporate both computer literacy and information literacy as essential components of students' education.

Taylor, Robert S. "Reminiscing About the Future: Professional Education and the Information Environment." *Library Journal* 104 (September 15, 1979): 1871–75.

A new educational framework for library science students is proposed, one that would integrate library science into the field of information science. Major problems for the new information environment are information imbalance, availability of information, information literacy, and the need to maintain a human aspect.

Trauth, E. M. "A College Curriculum for Information Literacy." *Education & Computing* 2 (no. 4, 1986): 251–58.

Offers an excellent compilation of literature relevant to the development of curricula designed to help prepare students for life in an information-based society. Contains forty-nine references.

_____. "Information Literacy Course: A Recommended Approach." In *Proceedings of NECC/5,* National Education Computing Conference, June 6–8, 1983, Baltimore, MD. Ames, IA: University of Iowa, Weeg Computer Center for NECC, 1983.

Discusses the need to go beyond computer literacy courses in order to educate students to respond to the demands of an information-intensive society. What is needed is a greater emphasis on information literacy, and an alternative course is described which is intended to promote the development of information literacy.

Turock, Betty J. *Public Library Services for Aging in the Eighties.* A 1981 White House Conference on the Aging Background Paper. Paper presented at the White House Conference on Aging (3rd), November 30–December 3, 1981, Washington, D.C. ED 215285.

Provides an overview of library and information services for older adults. Contains four major sections dealing with (1) information access, (2) education for lifelong learning, (3) information categories, and (4) management and training to provide public library services for the aging. The education section focuses on older adult learning and information education for service providers as well as a description of a public library model project which concentrates on training or educational methods to increase information literacy.

U.S. National Commission on Excellence in Education. *A Nation at Risk*. Washington, D.C.: Government Printing Office, 1983.

This document may be considered as the starting point for the information literacy movement as it currently exists, because the educational reforms it discussed and recommended omitted any role for libraries and thereby provoked a sharp reaction among librarians and educators.

Van Weering, B., A. Hartsuijker, and T. Zeelenberg. "From Computer Literacy to Information Literacy." Paper in *Computers in Education:* Proceedings of the IFIP TC 3, 4th World Conference, July 29–August 2, Norfolk, VA. Amsterdam, Netherlands: Elsevier, 1985.

Results are presented regarding the national project for the development of a curriculum on computer and information literacy for students and teachers of junior high schools in the Netherlands.

Wigersma, Helen. "Playing a Numbers Game." *Show-Me Libraries* 36 (October/November 1984): 23–25.

Discusses the problem of promoting library literacy and information literacy in a commuter-based college which exhibits an increasingly job-oriented educational structure. The author explores the relationship between high academic standards, a quality academic program, and library research. Attempts to establish whether or not commuter-based community colleges have a unique problem in requiring library-related assignments of their students as part of the learning process.

Zurkowski, Paul G. "The Library Context and the Information Context: Bridging the Theoretical Gap." *Library Journal* 106 (July 1981): 1381–84.

Discusses the impact of the "information business" on libraries and the need to improve the public's information literacy.

_____. "The Information Service Environment Relationships and Priorities. Related Paper No. 5." National Commission on Libraries and Information Science, Washington, D.C., 1974.

The relationship of the National Program for Library and Information Services to information literacy and the information industry are discussed. The traditional relations of libraries with the information industry are described and examples are given of situations where these historic roles are in transition. The author suggests that the top priority of the National Commission on Libraries and Information Science should be directed toward establishing a major national program to achieve universal information literacy by 1984. This may well be the earliest use of the term information literacy, although not in the fullest sense of the concept as developed in the 1980s.

Appendix:
Goals for American Education

* By the year 2000, every child will start school ready to learn.

* By the year 2000, the high school graduation rate will increase to at least 90 percent.

* By the year 2000, American students will leave grades four, eight, and twelve having demonstrated competency in challenging subject matter including English, mathematics, science, history, and geography; and every school in America will ensure that all students learn to use their minds well, so they may be prepared for responsible citizenship, further learning, and productive employment in our modern economy.

* By the year 2000, U.S. students will be the first in the world in science and mathematics achievement.

* By the year 2000, every adult American will be literate and will possess the knowledge and skills necessary to compete in a global economy and exercise the rights and responsibilities of citizenship.

* By the year 2000, every school in America will be free of drugs and violence and will offer a disciplined environment conducive to learning.

> — *Joint Statement by President George Bush and the Governors of the United States of America, February 26, 1990*

About the Contributors

Charles Curran is an associate professor at the College of Library and Information Science, University of South Carolina. He represents the Association for Library and Information Science Education in the National Forum on Information Literacy. He holds MLS and PhD. degrees from Rutgers, and has edited a book of readings honoring Ernest R. DeProspo, who taught at Rutgers SCILS from 1967 to 1983 (*Library Performance, Accountability and Responsiveness,* Ablex, 1990).

Prudence Ward Dalrymple is assistant professor at the University of Illinois Graduate School of Library and Information Science. She holds an MLS from Simmons and a PhD from the University of Wisconsin–Madison, and has worked in academic and medical libraries. She is a winner of the Association for Library and Information Science Education Doctoral Dissertation award, and was a Lilly Endowment Fellow (1989–90).

Howard M. Dess is physical sciences resource librarian at the Library of Science and Medicine at Rutgers. He holds a PhD in chemistry from the University of Michigan and an MLS from Rutgers.

Carol C. Kuhlthau is assistant professor at Rutgers SCILS. She has served on the American Library Association's Presidential Committee on Information Literacy, is past president of the Educational Media Association of New Jersey, and writes and lectures frequently on her research on students' information seeking behavior.

Major R. Owens, the first librarian elected to Congress (D-NY), has been a vigorous champion of libraries in the U.S. House of Representatives since 1982. Prior to that, he was a community coordinator for the Brooklyn Public Library, directed the community media library program at Columbia University, headed New York City poverty programs, and served in the New York Senate.

Karen Takle Quinn, recipient of the 1990 Distinguished Alumni Award and Fellow of the Institute of Information Scientists, is a product consultant for the strategic and marketing planning organization at IBM's Santa Teresa Laboratory in San Jose, California. Also at IBM, she was with the Corporate Technical Information Retrieval Service, served as systems analyst, database designer, and STL Librarian and Information/Learning Center Specialist. In the latter position, she pioneered the integration of the library with computer software and support functions, together with a learning center incorporating computer-aided instruction and technology. She has taught in San Jose's MLS program, and presents an electronically delivered course on information resources management.

Patricia Glass Schuman is president and co-founder of Neal-Schuman Publishers, Inc., and 1991–1992 president of the American Library Association. She has worked in public, school, and academic libraries, has taught at several library schools, and is a prolific writer and lecturer.

Jana Varlejs is director of Professional Development Studies and associate professor at Rutgers SCILS. She has edited the annual symposium proceedings since 1982.